Advance Praise for *Hooked on the Word*

"Many Christian believers are concerned about the inroads of New Age and Eastern philosophies into our Christian beliefs. For this reason the whole idea of meditation has been viewed with great skepticism. In doing so, however, we have also caused many Christian people to avoid any form of Christian meditation.

Ron Smith's book, *Hooked on the Word*, seeks to correct this distorted response. The focus of meditation for the Christian is to be on God and His word. The book rightly lifts up scripture as the central focus for the Christian and helps to show how we can both meditate and delight in the word in such a way that it becomes a means of grace. Not only will we benefit physically and psychologically from such meditation but there is clear evidence that relaxation both of the mind and of the body can help relieve stress and heal the body. Christians need to rediscover the value of biblical meditation and I believe that Ron Smith's book helps us to do this." **Archibald D. Hart, Ph.D.**
Dean
Professor of Psychology
Fuller Theological Seminary

"In this treatise on Biblical meditation, Ron Smith elucidates the basis for its' legitimacy in current Christian practice, and reviews the multiple benefits, spiritual, psychological, and physical, that can be expected to result from its consistent use. The medical aspects alone are intriguing and exciting in their potential for helping the believer."
D. Alec Lindley, M.D.
Contributing author,
New England Journal of Medicine

"This is a prophetic book regarding the Word of God, and it shows clearly how disrespect for it has brought a decline in literacy in the public schools of America and how respect for God's Word brings spiritual, intellectual, psychological and physical health. The reader will be stimulated, gripped with excitement, informed, encouraged and enabled to begin the walk that will lead to the joy and strength of meditation." **David E. Ross**
Missionary Statesman

"I was excited when I read your book on Biblical Meditation! I have experienced many of the benefits you describe from meditating daily on God's Word in my own life.

As a Christian Psychologist, I have found that there is no question that an individual that comes to counseling with an already well established pattern of meditating daily on God's word is much easier to help. The process is quite often shortened and they are much more open to hearing from God." **Carol Fosdick, Ph.D.**
Clinical Psychologist

"Ron Smith is a true Bible Scholar. But he is most of all a man of God. He knows God and walks with God. He takes us by the hand as readers to inspire us, instruct us, and illustrate the joy, fulfillment and blessing of Bible meditation.

Hooked on the Word is balanced and life-giving. I recommend it, especially for those preparing for missionary service." **Loren Cunningham**
Founder and President
Youth with a Mission

Hooked

on

the Word

Hooked On The Word

Changing Your Life Through

Bible Meditation

By Ron Smith

Hooked on the Word

Copyright © 1994 by Ron Smith

All Scripture References taken from the Revised Standard
Version unless noted.
ISBN 0-9641913-0-X
Library of Congress Catalog Card Number 94-060805

Printed in the United States of America

West Shore Books is a part of Youth with a Mission, Montana, P.O. Box 3000, Lakeside, Montana, USA, 59922.

Thank You

To Judy, who has put up with another time of writing obsessiveness.

To Bruce and Lanita Tibbett who cajoled people for money, typed letters, stuffed envelopes, marketed, read, fed and started a publishing company on half a shoestring to see this work completed.

To Geoff Benge, editor and work horse extraordinaire, also to Rob Penner, Bob Robinson and Tammie Barnett for line and copy editing. Thank you to Summit Design for the excellent cover design. Thank you to YWAM Publishing for your constructive advice and encouragement.

To the Executive Counsel, Base Counsel, and Group of Eleven at the Lakeside Base in Youth with a Mission, Montana who gave us space, encouragement and money.

To everybody who willingly labored through the manuscript and then gave us very helpful encouragement.

To two role models: 1. Thank you David Ross for exemplifying meditation to me in the early days in Korea. 2. Thank you Kay Lindley, mother of four great kids, who is up daily - before sunrise - meditating on the Word of God and interceding daily for Judy and for me.

Dedication

To Those Who Struggle

In 1987 a missionary researcher, Phil Parshall, surveyed 390 missionaries from over 30 different missions agencies. Parshall asked these missionaries what was their greatest spiritual struggle on the mission field. The *overwhelming primary struggle* which they mentioned was maintaining a consistent "devotional life."

Most evangelical and charismatic Christians that I know (whether they are on the mission field or off) would say a hardy "Amen!"

My purpose is to help you as one who has struggled with my own devotional life. At times, I still miss days meditating and reading my Bible - after 15 years in missions.

In fact, I wholeheartedly sign this dedication as-

Your Brother in the Common Struggle,
Ron Smith
Lakeside, Montana
May, 1994

Table of Contents

Introduction

> "What is the word when we come to the Bible? It
> is to meditate. We are to come to the Bible and
> meditate. That is what the old saints did. They
> meditated. They laid the Bible on the old fashioned
> chair, got down on the old scrubbed board floor and
> meditated on the Word. As they meditated, faith
> mounted....So be a Bible meditator. I challenge
> you to try it for a month and see how it works."[1]
> — A. W. Tozer

Unfortunately today, these words of A. W. Tozer seem
to fall on deaf ears. We have become preoccupied in the
church with doing things, getting caught up with activities,
rather than with being quiet before God and delighting in
His Word. Somehow, we have lost sight of the fact that
God places His highest value on the character and depth of
our relationship with Him and not on the sheer volume of
things we can accomplish for His kingdom. We have
grown so accustomed to measuring spiritual success in
terms of doing and accomplishing. Sitting in prayer or
silently contemplating the Word of God, for many, is akin
to "wasting time." Sometimes we feel it uses up valuable
time with little to show for it.

Jesus, however, had to remind the harassed Martha

that her sister had discovered what was the most important, most appropriate thing to do in the presence of the
Master—to sit at His feet (Luke 10:38-42).

When we look down through church history, we find
that those who have had the greatest impact in shaping the
church were those who did that very thing; they loved God
and His Word and they sat at His feet to learn from Him.
Augustine, Luther, Calvin, Wesley, Whitefield, Finney,
Moody and many other mighty men and women of God,
were people whose lives were marked and delineated by
their devotion to God's Word. They loved the Word, read
the Word, studied the Word, meditated on the Word,
preached the Word, lived according to the Word and they
would not attempt a thing for the kingdom of God unless
God Himself had first spoken clearly to them from His
Word. From our vantage point in time, we are able to look
back at the many things these people were able to accomplish for the kingdom and we marvel at their results.

Today, most of us can read adequately. If our Bible
study skills are undeveloped, there are numerous good
resources and books available to guide us in the process
of study. This is not the case when we consider meditating
on God's Word. There are few Christian books and resources on the subject.

Why is this?

The first reason we have already addressed: we are
too busy substituting activity for our relationship with the
Lord.

Second, the word "meditation" has taken on negative
connotations in the language of today's Christians. The
mere mention of the word sends pictures of saffron-robed

gurus sitting cross-legged on the floor, babbling mantras and drifting into trances, through the minds of most Christians. Or, if not pictures of gurus, then the concept of meditation is packed with baggage from the domain of the New Age movement. Meditation becomes synonymous with everything from self-improvement techniques to astral-projection. Such an approach, to use the cliche, is "throwing the baby out with the bath water."

In shrinking back from meditation, the church has created a spiritual vacuum. Spiritual vacuums are often filled by counterfeits. Alas, these counterfeits have captured the hearts and minds of millions. When we, in the church, should have been pondering the implications of the Bible to our daily lives and declaring the necessity of finding spiritual nourishment through meditating on the Word of God, we have instead cowered back, afraid of the very word meditation.

The idea, though, of meditating on the Word of God is firmly rooted in the Bible and is central to the lives of many of the people whose stories are recounted within its pages. Certainly, there is a corrupted form of meditation practiced by eastern religionists, New Age mystics, cultists and occultists alike. Opposite the counterfeits, there is a pure, holy, good and edifying form of meditation which the Bible sets forth and which today we call, Bible meditation.

It is time for Christians to reclaim the heritage we have surrendered in our fear and loathing of the word "meditation." It is time for us once again to become a people who delight in the Word of God and meditate on it day and night (Psalms 1:2).

A third reason meditation has fallen from favor in the church is guilt. We have tried so hard, so many times, to establish a regular devotional time with the Lord and have failed miserably. In the end, all we feel is guilt and shame over our lack of success. Thus, when we hear of our need to meditate on God's Word, we are neither ready nor willing to listen.

Of course, this cycle of guilt drives the frantic activity we often fall into. Activity becomes a way to placate our conscience and, hopefully, earn us some favor from God which just might outweigh the guilt we feel.

I have been a fellow-traveler on this road. My life has been marked by periods of guilt over my inability to establish a routine and successful quiet time with the Lord. I tried different approaches, different programs, different guide books and the like, but always with the same result—failure. That is when my eyes began to be opened to a truth I was missing. If I miss dinner, I do not feel guilty, I feel hungry! And that is how we should see our devotional time with the Lord. We are not plugging into a program, we are feeding our souls. If we miss our daily time with the Lord, we should feel spiritually hungry, not condemned. Guilt and condemnation are altogether the wrong reaction to missing our regular time with the Lord. Spiritual hunger is the correct response. We should hunger and thirst for our next time with the Lord. When we feel like this, we want to embrace God's Word more, not hang our heads and walk away in shame.

It is a simple truth, but it has set me free. Time with the Lord has become more of a joy to me, not an assignment powered by guilt. (I still miss days meditating and wish that I had not missed them.)

The great discovery I have made is Bible meditation. Bible meditation has invigorated my relationship with the Lord.

In the pages that follow, I want to help you discover Bible meditation. I want you to see that Bible meditation is not some new pseudo-psychological gimmick that we can employ to help improve the quality of our lives. Rather, I want you to see that meditating on the Word of God is a fundamental Judeo-Christian practice; one which, from the patriarchs of the Old Testament down through church history to today, men and women have used to feed their souls and deepen their walks with the Lord.

Most of all, in this book I want to show you how to *get hooked* and *stay hooked* on the Word of God.

[1] *How to Be Filled with the Holy Spirit*, A. W. Tozer, pages 56-57.

Ascribe to the Lord, O heavenly beings,
Ascribe to the Lord glory and strength.
Ascribe to the Lord the glory of his name;
Worship the Lord in holy array.
The voice of the Lord is upon the waters;
The God of glory thunders,
The Lord, upon many waters.
The voice of the Lord is powerful,
The voice of the Lord is full of majesty.
The voice of the Lord breaks the cedars,
The Lord breaks the cedars of Lebanon.
He makes Lebanon to skip like a calf, and
Sirion like a young wild ox.
The voice of the Lord flashes forth flames of fire.
The voice of the Lord shakes the wilderness,
The Lord shakes the wilderness of Kadesh.
The voice of the Lord makes the oaks to whirl,
And strips the forest bare;
And in his temple all cry, "Glory!"
The Lord sits enthroned over the flood;
The Lord sits enthroned as king for ever.
May the Lord give strength to his people!
May the Lord bless his people with peace!

Psalms 29

1

The Power of God's Word

"It's only a book! It's only a book!" shouted the professor. Rice paper pages fluttered around the classroom as the professor tore them from the black leatherbound Bible he was holding and tossed them into the air. The students in the introductory religion class sat in stunned silence. This was not what they had expected in their religion class.

This incident occurred not so long ago at a denominational college in the United States. This professor (who taught the New Testament) wanted to graphically get the point across to his students that they were embarking upon the study of just another book; a book of some spiritual value certainly, but a book, nonetheless, with printed and bound pages like every other book.

Unfortunately, the professor had lost sight of an important fact; God's Word does not just consist of letters printed on a page in black ink. Rather, each word, each sentence, each paragraph and each verse in the Bible is filled with the breath of God Himself. They convey God's heart and character to us. They are from God and, as such, are backed by the full power of the Father, Son and Holy Spirit. God's Word is not some puny, printed book, God's Word is powerful!

David knew this truth. "The voice of the Lord is powerful," he declared in Psalms 29. What is the Bible, but the voice of God recorded for all to read, ponder and gain spiritual understanding. David knew that if he made God's Word the center of his life, then God's power would follow. The most cursory study of David's life reveals this to be so. Whether he was standing before Goliath, killing a marauding lion or confronting King Saul, God's power was upon David.

Every Christian I know would like to experience God in the same way David did. We want to feel His power welling up within us as we face some deep crisis in our lives. We want to be emboldened by God as we wrestle with the enemy in spiritual warfare. We want to know God's peace when the trials of life buffet us. Well, the good news is, each of us can experience the presence of God like this in our everyday life.

God did not indiscriminately pour out His power on David as though David had no choice in the matter. The power of God was poured out on David because he sought the Lord. Day and night he meditated on God's Word. He delighted in God's Word. He read it, memorized it, sang it and constantly mulled it over in his mind as he went about his daily activities. In response, God released His power in David's life.

Like David, each of us can experience God's power. To do so, we need to make God's Word the center of our lives.

Making God's Word the center of our lives is what this book is all about. Before we discover how we go about making it such, we must first be totally convinced that His Word is powerful and that if we center in on that Word, read it, study it, meditate on it and absorb it into our hearts, then the release of God's power in our lives will follow.

The Power of God's Word at Work

Power to Bring New Life

Although he lived some sixteen hundred years ago, St Augustine is considered by most historians to be the church's most influential theologian. Prior to his conversion, though, Augustine lived a life of degradation and sin. In his book, *Confessions,* he recounts how one day, as he sat wondering about the direction of his life, he heard a child's voice singing out, "Take it and read it-take it and read it." Augustine goes on to say:

> I checked the force of my tears and rose to my feet being quite certain that I must interpret this as a Divine command to me that I must open the Bible and read the first passage which I should come upon....
> I snatched up the Bible, opened it and read in silence the passage upon which my eyes first fell. *[The passage was in Romans.]* 'Not in reveling and drunkenness, not in debauchery and licentiousness, not in quarreling and jealousy, but put on the Lord Jesus Christ and make no provision for the flesh to gratify its desires.' I had no wish to read further, there was no need to, for immediately as I had reached the end of this sentence it was as though my

> heart had been filled with the light of confidence
> and all the shadows of my doubt were swept away.[1]

Augustine was converted through reading 1 out of 32,000 verses in the Bible. He read that verse as though it was God's personal Word to him. He pondered that Word in his heart and then responded to it. As a result, he was gloriously converted. "My heart had been filled with light," he wrote of the experience and the church is theologically richer because of that experience.

There is power in God's Word!

Derek Prince had a similar experience. Prince was a philosopher who graduated top of his class from Cambridge University in England. During World War II, Prince was sent to North Africa to serve with the British Medical Corps. While there, never having read the Bible before, he decided to begin reading it through. His motivation to read the Bible did not come from a desire to know more about God, but rather came from a sense of obligation. The Bible was a great work of Hebrew philosophy and, as a philosopher, Derek Prince thought he should familiarize himself with it. However, as he read on through this book of Hebrew philosophy, he began to notice a change within himself. He began to feel that there was some great need in his life. His sense of intellectual superiority slowly began to subside. Finally, one balmy North African night, Derek Prince accepted Christ into his heart. He moved from death to life and his life was never again the same.

How was this change brought about? Through the power of God released into one man's heart as he began to read and contemplate the Word of God.

Several years ago, Open Air Campaigners, an evangelistic organization in New Zealand, directed a project called Operation Ezra. The point of the project was to attempt to evangelize New Zealand in a unique way. Small teams of six people each were recruited from around the world. The teams were then sent to the major cities of New Zealand. In those cities, they stood on the street corners and took turns reading the Bible, from Genesis to Revelation, for the benefit of passers- by.

A friend of mine, Mary Young, was on one of the teams in the city of Auckland. When Mary's turn came to read, she was to read Leviticus chapter 18 and the chapters following. In these chapters, the horrendous sins of the Egyptians and the Canaanites are catalogued: idolatry, unclean sexuality, violence and the list goes on and on for five whole chapters!

As Mary read through these chapters, a woman walking by became mesmerized by what she heard. God captured her attention. She thought about what she was hearing for a few minutes and then walked across to one of Mary's teammates and asked her, "As I hear this lady reading, I feel dirty. Is there anyone among you who can tell me how to get clean?" The Word of God had impacted her as she gave her attention to what she was hearing. As a result, right there on a busy street in Auckland, New Zealand, this woman gave her life to the Lord.

In 1975, I was teaching at a Christian high school. Dede, who had previously been a dancer in Paris, France, was also on the staff of the school. One day, I asked Dede how she had become a Christian. Her story was fascinating. One night, during the intermission, she walked into the bathroom of the club in which she was performing. There on the bathroom floor was half of a torn evangelistic tract. Dede picked up the piece of gospel tract and read it. The Bible truths printed on the tract particularly caught her attention. She could not get them out of her mind. She stood there in the bathroom mulling them over. As she did so, the eyes of her spiritual understanding were opened. She knew what she had to do and, right there, in the bathroom of a Parisian night club, Dede was gloriously converted.

How did this happen? It was simply the power of God's Word working in the life of someone who paused long enough to listen to it and consider its implications for her life.

Power to Perform Signs and Wonders

Don is a doctor friend of mine who has had a long ministry of healing and miracles. His meetings have regularly drawn crowds of up to five thousand people. During the early 1970's, he held monthly meetings in a church on the West Coast. Amazing and miraculous things happened during these meetings; people were healed of physical ailments, others were set free from bondages they had wrestled with and many people received salvation.

These meetings also attracted the attention of a group of theologians. They put Don's ministry under the microscope. They wanted to know where the power to do what Don was doing came from. Don was not surprised by their scrutiny of his ministry. Jesus, after all, had faced similar scrutiny during his earthly ministry.

One night, a group of these theologians decided to attend one of Don's meetings and see first-hand for themselves what went on in them. They assembled themselves in the front row. Don knew his ministry was on trial that night and he waited nervously in a back room as the crowd began to pack into the auditorium.

As he paced back and forth waiting for the service to begin, Don heard God speak to him. "Read ten passages of Scripture from the pulpit instead of preaching a sermon," the Lord whispered into his heart.

That is exactly what Don did. He opened his Bible and read from it. And when he had finished reading, a dead silence haunted the auditorium. Finally, after several minutes, the silence was broken by the wife of one of the church elders. From the back of the room she thundered a prophecy, "You have resisted my power. Why have you stood against my Word which has come through my servant?"

With that, things broke open. People began to receive healing, others fell to their knees on the floor to repent and receive salvation, and still others were delivered and set free from various bondages. The power of God broke loose!

And what had Don done? He had simply been obedient to the Lord and read ten passages of Scripture to the audience. As the audience pondered the implications of those verses to their lives, God saw fit to say "Amen" to His Word by releasing His power. Many people's needs were meet that night as a result.

In 1983, a young Korean woman lay writhing like a snake on the floor of her Bible school classroom. The teacher walked over to where she lay and, seeing she was demonically oppressed, instructed another young woman in the class to read Ephesians 1:15-23 to her.

The young woman did as she was instructed and read the passage to the demonically oppressed woman, but nothing happened. She continued to writhe on the floor. So she read it through a second time. Still nothing happened. Then, a third time, she read the passage to the oppressed woman. This time, the power of God was released. The demonic bondage was broken. The young Korean woman stopped writhing and sat up. She was set free by the power of God.

A missionary to Latin America, who led hundreds of people to the Lord during the 1950's, '60's and '70's, found the same to be true. When converts came to him with demonic problems, he would tell them to go and read passages from the Bible, meditate on them, memorize them and recite them to themselves. As they followed through on his instructions, many of these new converts testified to being set free from their demonic bondage.

There is power in God's Word. Power to bring about miracles of healing and deliverance in the lives of people.

God's Word Empowers and Creates

Eric Lidell was an Olympic gold medal winning runner about whom the movie, *Chariots of Fire,* was made. Eric Lidell also practiced a time of daily Bible meditation in his devotional life. No doubt, the release of the power of God he experienced was a result of that meditation. It allowed him to become not only an Olympic champion, but also an effective missionary, greatly loved by the

Chinese people among whom he served.

There is also Charles Wesley, brother of John Wesley the founder of the Methodist church. Not only was Charles Wesley one of the church's greatest hymn-writers, he also spent time each day in God's Word. The hymns he created reflect his devotion to the Word of God. One writer says Charles Wesley's hymns are like an "enormous sponge, filled to saturation with Bible words, Bible similes, Bible metaphors, Bible stories, Bible themes."[2] His hymns contain 2,500 verses of Scripture from every book of the Bible except Nahum and Philemon.

Not only did Charles Wesley experience great power to create and write some of the church's most enduring hymns as a result of his devotion to the Word of God, but those hymns in turn touched the lives of others with the power of God.

A story is told of Charles and John Wesley going late one night to pray with an unsaved woman who was being harassed by demons. The two brothers spoke with the woman and then they began to sing some of Charles' Scripture laden hymns. They sang on into the morning hours and, by the time they left, the demons had stopped harassing the woman and she had given her life to the Lord.

George Mueller was a man led by God to start a number of orphanages in England during the last century. Before ministry, though, Mueller believed God had shown him that his first call was to be sure that his soul was happy in the Lord. And the way God had shown him to be "happy in his soul," Mueller believed, was through a daily practice of Bible meditation.

"God showed me that I should go to his Word just to get one thing to chew on early in the morning. This is not something for my own ministry but something for me personally that I would be nourished."[3]

History testifies to the tremendous impact that this time of Bible meditation had on the ministry of George Mueller. Through his ministry, many orphanages were established in which hundreds of orphans were fed and housed and in which they heard about a God who loved them.

Spreads Throughout the Earth

In 1978, a missionary was riding in a taxi cab through the streets of Calcutta, India. As she stared out the window of the taxi, she noticed four teenage thugs standing on a street corner. Sensing someone needed to witness to these boys, but fearing for her safety if she left the taxi, she found a Scripture tract in her handbag. She rolled down the window of the taxi and threw out the tract. The tract came to rest on the pavement near the teenage thugs and one of them, Ambi, went over to pick it up.

Ambi was from a tribe of people that had no written language, but during his time in Calcutta he had learned to read and write English. He stood on the crowded street and read the Scripture tract. Tears filled his eyes as he did so. The words he read pierced his heart. There on that dirty, bustling Calcutta street, Ambi turned his life over to the Lord.

Ambi's story does not finish there. He went on to attend university where he studied medieval English literature. After he graduated, he traveled to the United States where, with five other people, he developed a written form of the language for his tribe and then translated the New Testament. Living Bibles International published 10,000 copies of this New Testament and people from thirty nations contributed to the publishing costs. Finally, a copy of the New Testament was delivered to every household in Ambi's tribe.

How did all this happen? It happened when the power of God was released in one young man's life through his reading the Word of God printed on a simple Scripture tract.

God's Word has great power!

The Word of God Brings Fulfillment

Matthew Henry was a Puritan Bible expositor. His life was consumed with the Word of God. Daily he read, studied, prayed over and meditated upon the Word of God and the great insights he discovered are recorded for us in his commentaries.

On his death bed, his life's work complete, Matthew Henry turned to his friend, Mr. Illage and said, "You have been used to taking notice of the statements of dying men, this is mine. A life spent in the service of God and communion with Him is the most comfortable and pleasant life that one can live in the present world."[4]

Matthew Henry found great fulfillment and contentment through centering his life around the Word of God. Compare Matthew Henry's last words to those of Voltaire.

Voltaire was an 18th century French rationalist. During his life, he penned many scathing tracts which rebuked the church; claiming, among other things, that within 100 years Christianity would be a thing of the past and that the Bible would be seen as a mere fairy tale.

At Voltaire's death bed, his condition became so bad that his unbelieving associates were afraid to even approach him. Finally, Voltaire turned to face the wall and cried out, "I must die abandoned of God and of men." After watching him die, his nurse said, "I would not for all of the wealth of Europe, I would never ever want to be near the bed of a dying infidel again, the experience was so horrible!"

How different was Voltaire's experience from Matthew Henry's. The one filled with joy and contentment, the other filled with anguish and despair. And what made the difference? The attitude of these two men to the Word of God-The one loved it, the other despised it.

There is also a fascinating footnote to Voltaire's story, one that again speaks to the mighty power of God's Word. Voltaire had lived in a house in Geneva and exactly one hundred years after his death, the British and Foreign Bible Society set up their new Geneva office in Voltaire's house. Not only did they move into Voltaire's house, but they also used his printing press to print Bibles! Nothing can stop the power of God's Word.

The writer to the Hebrews tells us that the Word of God is "quick and powerful" (Hebrews 4:12 KJV). It is powerful enough to lead the unrepentant to repentance, to meet the needs of the most needy heart, as well as, to bring forth healing and miracles in the lives of people. It can bring joy, comfort, challenge, even correction to a person. It is the most powerful Word in the universe and all that is needed for that power to be released is for men and women to apprehend God's Word in their hearts and minds. For those who do so, like David of old, their testimony will be "God's Word is powerful!"

The person who takes God's Word seriously and begins to regularly read, study and meditate on the Bible, can expect that Word to touch a number of areas in their life.

[1] *The Confessions*, Augustine of Hippo.
[2] *Christian History Magazine, Vol.1 no.2,* Frank Baker.
[3] Quoted in *Alone With God*, Campbell McAlpine, Bethany House Publishers.
[4] *Voices From the Edge of Eternity*, Myers.

Action Steps
Chapter One

1. Think back on how God's Word was involved in your salvation experience.

2. Discuss this with a friend or classmate. Listen to his or her story as well.

3. Start taking 15 minutes per day to simply sit down and relax in a quiet and uninterrupted place. (You may be surprised at how difficult this is at first.)

But as for you, continue in what you have learned and have firmly believed, knowing from whom you learned it and how from childhood you have been acquainted with the sacred writings which are able to instruct you for salvation through faith in Christ Jesus. All scripture is inspired by God and profitable for teaching, for reproof, for correction, and for training in righteousness, that the man of God may be complete, equipped for every good work.

2 Timothy 3:14-16

2

God's Word at Work
in Our Lives

Carol is a friend who became involved in a religious cult. The cult emphasized meditation and, as Carol progressed in her meditation, she was instructed to say certain things while meditating. Carol felt uncomfortable doing this and instead reached back into her Catholic upbringing. She began reciting over and over to herself the Scriptural prayers she remembered. One Scriptural prayer she found herself repeating more than any other was, "Lord Jesus Christ, have mercy on me a sinner."

As Carol continued to recite prayers to herself, over a period of time, God began to open her eyes to the need for her to repent and give her life to the Lord. Finally, she yielded to the prompting of the Holy Spirit and received new life in Christ.

Today, Carol is a missionary sharing the message of the gospel to a spiritually needy world.

While I was pastor of a church during the late 1970's, a man in the congregation broke down and began to weep uncontrollably right in the middle of one of my Sunday morning sermons. Thinking the sermon had somehow touched his heart, I sought the man out after the service. To my delight, he had given his life to the Lord right in the middle of the sermon. So I asked him which part of the sermon had spoken to him. "It was nothing in your sermon," he replied. Instead, he had turned to a passage from the Old Testament, a different passage to the one I was preaching from and began to read. As he read, his eyes were opened to his need for salvation. So compelling were the emotions that came with this realization, that he began to weep as he surrendered his heart and experienced God's new life flow into him.

Both of these people experienced the life-giving power of the Word of God at work in their lives. God's Word, in conjunction with the prompting of the Holy Spirit, had done its work in their lives; it had drawn attention to their need of salvation and delivered them into new life in Christ. As Peter puts it, they had been "born anew, not of perishable seed but of imperishable, through the living and abiding Word of God" (1 Peter 1:23).

In 2 Timothy 3:14-17, Paul lays out several other functions that the Word of God performs in the believer's life. He tells us that Scripture is able to lead us to salvation through faith in Christ. As well, he points out that the Word of God produces discipleship in our lives; it corrects us, rebukes us and trains us to be righteous.

God's Word Produces Discipleship

> If you continue in my word, you are truly my
> disciples, and you will know the truth, and the truth
> will make you free. (John 8:31-32)

Notice the phrase Jesus uses here, *continue in my Word*. Discipleship is not something to be learned in a one or two month "discipleship program." Discipleship is a lifelong process. Discipleship requires that we continue in His Word.

But what does this mean?

Continuing in the Word means that we keep on reading it, studying it, meditating on it and listening to the preaching of the Word. Beyond this, to truly continue in the Word means that we must *obey* it!

James tells us that we should be "doers of the word, and not hearers only, deceiving yourselves" (James 1:22).

Consider the metaphor of the mirror which James also uses in his book. When I get up in the morning and go to the mirror to look into it, it is as though the mirror talks back to me. It says, "Good morning Ron. You do not look so good this morning. If you want to be acceptable to people today, you need to shower, shave, brush your hair and clean your teeth."

I then have a choice. I can accept what the mirror has revealed to me and clean myself up for the day ahead or I can say, "So what! I like looking this way." However, if I take this second approach, I have not allowed the mirror to do its proper work.

God's Word is a mirror to us. Through reading, studying and meditating on the Word, God reveals areas to us that need to be dealt with and brought into submission to His Word. When we look at the mirror and change, God's Word has done its work.

Of course, we can choose to hear His Word and not obey it, but as James has already pointed out, we are deceiving ourselves. When we hear the Word, but do not obey it, we are walking in disobedience and rebellion, not discipleship.

We will never outgrow the need for God's Word to be a mirror to us. All the days we are on this earth, God is perfecting us for the kingdom to come. So the process of discipleship continues throughout our lives and thus Jesus' admonition to us to continue in His Word.

God's Word Corrects and Rebukes Us

After David had become king of Israel and chosen Jerusalem to be his capital, he wanted to bring the Ark of the Covenant (the Old Testament symbol of God's presence) into the city. 1 Chronicles documents the venture.

> And David and all Israel were making merry before God with all their might, with song and lyres and harps and tambourines and cymbals and trumpets. And when they came to the threshing floor of Chidon, Uzzah put out his hand to hold the ark, for the oxen stumbled. And the anger of the Lord was kindled against Uzzah; and he smote him because he put forth his hand to the ark; and he died there before God. (1 Chronicles 13:8-10)

The zealousness of David and his men in bringing the ark to Jerusalem is remarkable. They were so joyous, so celebratory and so wrong in the way they went about things.

After the incident, David found correction by reading the book of Numbers where it says only the Levites should carry the ark. So David called the Levites together and said to them regarding what had happened, "Because you did not carry it (the ark) the first time, the Lord our God broke forth upon us, because we did not care for it in the way that is ordained" (1 Chronicles 15:13).

In other words, the Word of God rebuked and corrected David regarding his former attempt to take [the Ark] of the Covenant to Jerusalem.

To "rebuke" means to give "sharp criticism." When God rebukes us through His Word, it is always with a view toward a positive change in our lives. There is always a redemptive goal attached to any correction God needs to bring. It may not always be pleasant. We may need to exercise humility and ask forgiveness of God and others, but if we persevere, we will reap great benefit in our lives.

For many years, I held adamantly, legalistically to the belief that Christians were obliged to turn over 10% of their gross income to God's work. Wherever I went, I presented that message forcefully, but then God rebuked me from His Word. I was theologically out of balance and needed correction. As I meditated on Hebrews chapters 7 and 8, my eyes were opened to the fact that the whole levitical system came to an end with Christ. When that system ended, the tithe ended also. Some New Testament churches practiced tithing, others did not.

Having had my eyes opened to this truth, I had to repent of the way I had preached the law wrongly and had condemned other Christians.

But the rebuke of God's Word brought liberation to my soul; liberation from the bonds of legalism, liberation from striving to earn God's favor by giving 10% of my income to God's work and seeking to get as many others as I could to do the same.

Of course, it is easy sometimes to fall into condemnation when we receive a rebuke from the Lord, but that is not God's purpose. He wants to see us set free in those areas He brings to our attention. In calling attention to those things, God is asking us to surrender them to Him. And if we surrender them to Him, His Word promises that He will give us the power to deal with those situations.

God's Word Trains Us to Be Righteous

> But now the righteousness of God has been manifested apart from law, although the law and the prophets bear witness to it, the righteousness of God through faith in Jesus Christ for all who believe. For there is no distinction; since all have sinned and fall short of the glory of God, they are justified by his grace as a gift, through the redemption which is in Christ Jesus
> (Romans 3:21-24).

Paul clearly shows here that righteousness is something God gives to every person who, by faith, accepts Christ into their life. Paul also reminds Timothy that God's Word trains us in righteousness. So, righteousness is both something given to us by God and something we live out in our daily life. John further illuminates this when he says:

> Little children, let no one deceive you. He who does right is righteous, as he [Christ] is righteous.
>
> (1 John 3:7)

It is in doing what is right that the Word of God trains us. As we have already pointed out, God's Word produces discipleship, as well as, corrects and rebukes us. But what does discipleship and receiving correction from the Lord lead to? They lead to righteous living—doing what is right in the sight of God and our fellow human beings. So when the Word of God fulfills these functions in our lives, it is training us in righteous living. As well, daily reading, studying and meditating on God's Word shows us new insights into how we ought to live our lives on a daily basis.

We must be careful, though, that we do not get caught in the trap of trying, in our *own* strength, to be righteous in order to win favor from the Lord. God has already shown us favor by sending Christ to die for our sins. Through faith in Him, God has given His righteousness to us. Thus, we do not have to try in our strength to live righteously, but rather we are to let God's righteousness flow into our daily living. Guiding us in how to do this is one of the functions of God's Word in our lives.

God's Word is a Tool in Spiritual Warfare

> Again, the devil took him to a very high mountain,
> and showed him all the kingdoms of the world and
> the glory of them; and he said to him, "All these I
> will give you, if you will fall down and worship
> me." Then Jesus said to him, "Begone, Satan! for
> it is written, 'You shall worship the Lord your God
> and him only shall you serve.'" Then the devil left
> him, and behold, angels came and ministered to
> him. (Matthew 4:8-11)

This third temptation of Jesus by the devil is abstracted from the complete account of the events which Matthew records for us in chapter 4 of his gospel. We like to refer to the full account as the "Temptation of Jesus." However, it is more than just a record of Jesus being tempted—it is an account of Jesus engaged in spiritual warfare with the devil. Three times the devil came to Jesus and tried to tempt Him to sin. Each time Jesus' response was the same. Each time He quoted Scripture back at the devil until, finally, the devil gave up and left Him.

In spiritual warfare, Jesus' weapon of choice to fight off Satan was the Word of God.

I believe God allowed this account of Jesus' temptation to be recorded in His Word to serve as an example for us today. Like Jesus, our Master Teacher, we are to use the Word of God as a weapon in our spiritual warfare. However, to use the Word effectively, we must know it. We get to know God's Word by reading it, studying it and daily meditating on it. When we do this, we will be armed and ready to stand against the wiles of the devil.

God's Word Creates

The book of Genesis declares that God created the heavens and the earth. How did He create them? By His spoken Word! God's written Word contains the same power as His spoken Word. We have already explored this fact in the previous chapter.

However, as we meditate on God's Word and absorb it into our lives, it becomes a creative source of power for us. The most obvious expression of this creative power is in the work of the artist. Down through the ages, men and women have sought to express the truths of God's Word in works of sculpture, in painting, in music, in dance, in drama and a myriad of other forms of artistic expression.

Whether it be the great hymns of the church, the magnificent stained glass windows of a cathedral, the throbbing beat of a modern Christian band or the gripping adventure of a good Christian fiction story; they are all creative attempts to share the power, truth and beauty of God and His Word. For those of us who are Christians, they move our heart to love God more and for those who do not know God, they hold out the promise of His love for them.

Not all of us are artistic in this manner, but that does not mean we are devoid of creative power. We may simply express our creativity in different ways. Most of us have encountered experiences where we did not know how to deal with a situation or solve a problem. So we prayed and committed it to the Lord. As we churned the situation around in our minds, God called to mind something we had read in His Word. Suddenly connections were made, we could see how to solve our problem, we knew how to deal with the situation and away we went. That, too, is the creative power of the Word at work in our lives.

We are made in the image of God. We are made with the ability to be creative. The power source that God has made available to us for creativity is His Word.

All of the power of God's Word and the function of His Word at work in our lives is premised upon one thing: that we become actively involved with His Word on a regular and ongoing basis.

Imagine you are afflicted with a serious, life-threatening illness; your body is weak and wracked with pain. There is a potent medicine available that will quickly relieve your symptoms and return you to good health. The doctor has prescribed the medicine for you and you now have a small bottle of capsules on your bedside table. What are you going to do next? Are you going to continue lying there feeling miserable and stare at the medicine? Or are you going to open the bottle, take out the required dosage of capsules and swallow them?

Of course, you are going to take the capsules. Once swallowed, the medicine contained in the capsules will make you feel better.

The strongest medicine in the world does you no good unless you ingest it into your body. Only then can the medicine's power do its healing work in your body.

So, too, with God's Word. It has the power to make us spiritually whole people. However, it can only do its work in our lives when we take the time to ingest it. The best way to ingest God's Word is through reading it regularly, studying it often and meditating on it daily.

Most know how to read and study the Word, but many are unfamiliar with how to meditate regularly on God's Word. By the time you have finished reading this book, you will have gained enough information, insight and inspiration to make a regular time of meditation on God's Word your daily habit.

Action Steps
Chapter Two

1. Inventory your present relationship with your Bible.
       a.I spend_____ minutes every day in my Bible.
       b.This makes me feel_____ about my relationship with God.
       c.Discuss this with a friend or classmate.

2. The one thing I wish that I could improve about my Bible Study and meditation is...

3. I have meditated (distinguished from reading) on God's Word before. Yes or No.

4. Continue relaxing 15 minutes per day in a quiet uninterrupted place.

Blessed is the man
who walks not in the counsel of the wicked,
nor stands in the way of sinners,
nor sits in the seat of scoffers;
but his delight is in the law of the Lord,
and on his law he meditates day and night.
He is like a tree planted by streams of water,
that yields its fruit in its season,
and its leaf does not wither.
In all he does, he prospers.

The wicked are not so,
but are like chaff which the wind drives away.
Therefore the wicked will not stand in the judgement,
Nor sinners in the congregation of the righteous;
for the Lord knows the way of the righteous,
but the way of the wicked will perish.

Psalms 1

3

Delighting in God's Word

Right at the outset of the Psalms, David defines the blessed person as one who delights in the law of the Lord. It is an important theme for David. So much so that he repeats the same message several times over in Psalms 119. He says:

> "In the way of thy testimonies I delight as much as in all riches" (verse 14).
> "I will delight in thy statutes, I will not forget thy Word" (verse 16).
> "Thy testimonies are my delight, they are my counselors" (verse 24).
> "Lead me in the path of thy commandments, for I delight in it" (verse 35).
> "For I find my delight in thy commandments, which I love" (verse 47).
> "Their heart is gross like fat, but I delight in thy law" (verse 70).
> "Let thy mercy come to me, that I may live, for thy law is my delight" (verse 77).
> "If thy law had not been my delight, I should have perished in my affliction" (verse 92).

What does David mean when he says he delights in God's Word? The dictionary defines delighting in something as that thing becoming a cause or source of great pleasure for us. In this case, God's Word was that great source of pleasure for David.

Most of us have experienced, at some time or another, being away from home and getting a letter from someone we love. Perhaps it is a girl friend or a boy friend or a parent or a brother or a sister, or perhaps a close friend. When the letter arrives, we tear it open and read it. And then read it again. And again. When we have finished reading it, we do not crumple it up and toss it in the garbage. Instead, we neatly fold it and put it in a safe place. Why? Because receiving and reading the letter brought us much pleasure. It stirred up pleasant memories of home and of the person who wrote us the letter. Later, we want to take the letter out again and delight in it some more. We want it to be a further source of pleasure to us. So we keep the letter and re-read it often.

That is what David meant when he talked about delighting in God's Word. He is talking about making God's Word a great source of pleasure. So much so that we would constantly want to read it and ponder its implications in our hearts.

For David, the law of the Lord meant the first five books of the Bible. He delighted in those books. He meditated on them day and night, and he was rewarded with deep insights into the nature and character of God and how he was to relate to Him. These insights form the basis for many of David's psalms, among them Psalms 1.

It is interesting to note that Psalm 1, the introductory psalm to the book of Psalms, is basically a declaration of the importance of meditating on God's Word. David declares the person who delights in and meditates upon the law of the Lord to be blessed. He also goes on to compare the person who meditates to a strong and healthy tree.

> He is like a tree planted by streams of water, that yields its fruit in its season, and its leaf does not wither. In all that he does, he prospers.
>
> (Psalms 1:3)

Watching a tree grow is not a very exciting way to pass the time of day. A tree's growth is almost imperceptible on a day-to-day basis. But go away and come back in two years. You will see that tremendous growth has occurred in the tree. That growth has occurred in imperceptible daily bursts as the roots of the tree have drawn up nutrients from the soil.

The huge Sequoia trees in California's Redwood forests are remarkable specimens of nature. Yet no one has ever watched a Sequoia tree grow even an inch. Over the course of many hundreds of years we can not deny the fact that they have grown from small seeds to mighty trees.

The Bible meditator is like one of those Sequoia trees. Ten to twenty minutes of Bible meditation will not suddenly make us spiritually mature and sensitive, but ten to twenty minutes a day spread out over a period of time will bring great growth and change to our spiritual lives. Like a giant Sequoia tree, growth for the Bible meditator requires day-by-day, week-by-week feeding on God's Word.

Psychologist Dr. Paul Meier of the Minirth-Meier Clinic in Dallas, Texas, states that he has observed spiritual and emotional growth in people as a result of meditation. It takes time to occur, he points out, taking on average about three years of consistent meditation before such sustained growth is truly evident.

Everything of value, including the practice of Bible meditation, takes time to develop and even more time before the spiritual growth benefits are evident to ourselves and to others. In our instant society, this is not always a comforting truth, but it is a truth, nonetheless. A truth that David knew well. Years of his life were invested into delighting in and meditating upon the Word of God and the results were evident in his life.

David goes on to tell us in Psalms 1 that the Bible meditator is like a tree "planted by streams of water." Not just a stream of water, but streams of water. Often, when there are many streams of water running together, they form a swamp or a marsh.

Perhaps you have had the opportunity to visit some of the swamps in Florida. If you have, the first thing you probably noticed was how green, lush and alive everything appeared. Saw grass, wild orchids and ferns covered the saturated ground. Also, up from the midst of all this lush growth soared tall Cypress trees. These trees flourish in the swamp environment. With the ever abundant supply of water and nutrients they grow strong and tall. And that, David tells us, is what the Bible meditator is like, a tree planted by streams of water, able to draw nourishment from the Word of God. That nourishment allows the meditator to grow strong and mature in his spiritual life.

Then David continues on to tell us that the tree "yields its fruit in its season."

A banana tree produces an abundance of fruit, but it does not produce that fruit by simply reciting to itself, "I'm a banana tree, I'm going to make bananas." Bananas are produced naturally as the tree grows and is nourished. Fruit is the natural consequence of the process of growth and development that occurs in the tree. As a result, when the season is right, the banana tree bears fruit.

For the Bible meditator, the process of spiritual growth that occurs with ongoing Bible meditation produces fruit in his or her life. That fruit is often expressed in the form of spiritual character as it was in the life of David. It is that same fruit that can nourish the lives of others.

Then, on this tree that David compares the Bible meditator to, "Its leaf does not wither." When the leaves of a tree wither, it is a sure sign that the tree is not getting enough nourishing water from the ground. The tree is dry and if it finds no nourishment, it will die.

The Bible meditator should not experience dryness in his spiritual life. The daily nourishment he draws from the Word of God will keep his spiritual life dynamic and fresh. We speak often and openly in the church today about going through dry periods in our spiritual lives. There may be those times when God, in the process of teaching and training us, allows us to experience such a dry period. For the most part, though, these dry periods may occur because of neglect and poor planning.

Suppose we want to plant an apple tree so that when it has grown we can enjoy its fruit. So we plant the seed in the ground. Do we then sit back and wait for the apples to appear? No. To do so shows a lack of understanding on our part. As a result of our lack of understanding, we end up neglecting the tree. If we fail to correctly fertilize and water the apple tree, it will not produce large and healthy fruit. As anyone who has planted an apple tree knows, the tree must be nurtured. It must be regularly fertilized, watered and protected from pests and frost. With such nurture, the apple tree will grow strong and produce sweet, ripe apples for all to enjoy.

Bible meditation is a nutrient we need if we are to experience growth in our spiritual lives. Our failure to plan for the adequate nurture of our spiritual lives causes growth and development to be stifled, allowing long periods of spiritual dryness to creep into our lives.

Bible meditation, though, is not some ritualistic activity we put ourselves through. It is a two way activity. It is planting God's Word in our heart and then allowing Him to release the power of that Word into our lives. That is God's part. When, like the tree, we do our part by drawing in and absorbing the Word of God into our hearts, then God will cause growth to occur.

In essence, then, meditation is a two way relationship; it is fellowship with God.

Scripture records two major points of failure in David's life. Both of them occurred when David neglected his fellowship with the Lord. His first failure was committing adultery with Bathsheba and then trying to cover his tracks by having her husband, Uriah, killed. The second failure was that of numbering the people of Israel against God's will. I am sure if David were around today for us to ask him why he did these things, he would say it was because of a lapse in his meditating and communing with God. The leaves on his once healthy tree had withered. His relationship with the Lord had become dry and, as a result, he fell into sin.

Thus, when David declares meditating on the Word of God to be of paramount importance in the life of a child of God, he knows full well, from positive and negative experience, the absolute truth of what he is saying. He knows the importance of being like a tree and letting his roots go deep into the Word of God to draw in spiritual nourishment. David delighted in the Word of God and God raised him up to be a leader of his people.

But David is not the only dynamic leader in the Bible who knew the importance of and practiced Bible meditation.

Joshua

> Only be strong and very courageous, being careful to do according to all the law which Moses my servant commanded you; turn not from it to the right hand or to the left, that you may have good success wherever you go. This book of the law shall not depart out of your mouth, but you shall meditate on it day and night, that you may be careful to do according to all that is written in it; for then you shall make your way prosperous, and then you shall have good success. Have I not commanded you? Be strong and of good courage; be not frightened, neither be dismayed; for the Lord your God is with you wherever you go. (Joshua 1:7-9)

After Moses died, God raised up a new man to be in charge-Joshua. He was to lead Israel across the Jordan river and into the promised land. Along the way they would face the barbaric Canaanites. These cruel people sacrificed their first-born children and then placed their sacrificed bones in an earthen jar that was then built into the walls of their homes. Their wickedness had offended God and Joshua was to bring God's judgment against them. He was to lead the army of Israel to conquer and annihilate the Canaanites. It was a huge task that Joshua faced.

As the Lord called Joshua to undertake this task, he also promised him success. "No man shall be able to stand before you all the days of your life; as I was with Moses, so I will be with you; I will not fail you or forsake you" (Joshua 1:5). It was a great promise, but perhaps more interesting is how God directs Joshua to attain this promise. As Francis Schaeffer has noted[1], even though Joshua had served faithfully beside Moses for forty years, the Lord did not tell him to remember all Moses had done and think about it. Instead, God commanded Joshua to search out for himself from Scripture the wisdom he would need to fulfill the task. "This book of the law shall not depart out of your mouth, but you shall meditate on it day and night, that you may be careful to do according to all that is written in it (Joshua 1:8)." If he would do this, then God would be with him always and he would have good success.

Before anything else, God called Joshua to have an ongoing devotional life with meditation as a priority. Day and night he was to meditate on the Word of God but that did not mean he was to just sit and cogitate. Instead, he was to meditate on God's Word in order to obey it himself and enjoy God. He was also called to lead the people in obedience to it.

God calling Joshua to undertake all that he wanted him to accomplish, while at the same time commanding him to be constantly meditating on the Word of God, raises an interesting question. How was Joshua supposed to accomplish both of these seemingly full-time tasks?

The apostle Paul tells us in 2 Corinthians 10:5 that we should take captive every thought to make it obedient to Christ. That is what God was asking Joshua to do. He was to make his mind—his very being—captive to God's Word. His heart and mind were to be completely focused in on obedience to the Word of God. He was to delight in God's Word, mull it over in his mind and open his heart to receive new levels of understanding from God regarding his Word and how he should obey it. This process was to continue alongside doing the things God had asked Joshua to accomplish. This constant meditation was designed by God to provide Joshua with the wisdom he needed to accomplish the task.

Now this was a very different training approach from the physical, intellectual and tactical training today's military leaders receive. By staying true to all that God had commanded him, Joshua experienced great success in leading Israel to claim the land God had promised them. Supernaturally, Joshua led the people across the Jordan river. He conquered Jericho, Ai and Bethel. He saw God stop the sun and moon in mid-heaven. And the book of Joshua chapters 11 and 12 list thirty-one kings that he and his company conquered. Joshua accomplished all God had asked him to accomplish and Joshua 21:43-45 declares that God honored all the promises He had made to Joshua and Israel as a result. They, along with Joshua, prospered.

It is obvious that daily meditating on the Word of God shaped the life and character of both David and Joshua. Both of them became great leaders of their people. Everything they did prospered. That is not to say that they never stumbled, but that God used both of them in a dynamic way. The prerequisite God set for them was that they meditate on His Word.

The experience of Joshua and David is not just for God's chosen leaders, it is for all Christians. All that Joshua and David did was rooted in fellowship with God and the basis of that fellowship was meditating on the Word of God. God's instruction to Joshua that he should meditate on God's Word day and night is also for us today. As David points out, we should delight in God's Word. It should be a source of great pleasure to us. When it becomes that source of pleasure, we will enjoy a healthy, vibrant, mature and prosperous relationship with God; just as David and Joshua did.

[1] *Joshua and Clausewitz: A Brief Study of Leadership*, Colonel David Hansen, (1993).

Action Steps
Chapter Three

1. Discuss your favorite food with a friend. Take note of your internal responses to that food as you think of it and discuss it. Ask your friend his or her favorite food. Note the non-verbal responses from your friend as he or she describes his or her favorite food.

God wants us to respond to his Word the same way that we respond to our favorite foods. The word "delight" is related to delicious. God's Word should be "delicious" to us.

The best thing we can do is to pray that God will cause our hunger for His Word to grow, if this is not the case.

2. Continue relaxing 15 minutes every day.

4

Attitudes, Objects and Effects

Charles Spurgeon, the stirring British preacher of the last century, had this to say regarding the Word of God.

> I might also say that the major part of the Word of God is still in that condition: it is still an Eldorado unexplored, a land whose dust is gold.[1]

God's Word is an Eldorado, where nuggets of wisdom and diamonds of truth abound. It is a place that each Christian can explore and gather for themselves all that is precious to be found there. Unfortunately, for many Christians it is a place that remains unexplored. If we are willing to go in search of the riches of God's Word, then one of the greatest means at our disposal is Bible meditation.

In the previous chapter, we observed the process of spiritual growth that occurs in the life of the Bible meditator. Such growth occurs as a direct result of our exploration of God's Word. This growth can also be defined in terms of attitude, objects and effects. Thus we can say of Bible meditating, that spiritual growth occurs when the meditator approaches God and His Word with the *right attitude* focused on the *right objects*. When this is done, the meditator experiences the *proper effects* of meditation in his or her life.

The Proper Attitude Toward God and His Word

In discussing the proper attitude toward God and His Word, I am not talking about positive thinking or psychological trickery that gets us in the mood to meditate on the Bible. The psalmist makes it plain that before we even begin to meditate, we need to have the proper attitude. That proper attitude, he points out, consists of four things: loving God's Word and desiring to have him speak to us through it, submission to God's Word, commitment to God's Word and obedience to God's Word.

Loving God's Word and Desiring to Have Him Speak through It

1 Samuel 3 records the story of the first time the Lord spoke to Samuel. At first, the young boy ran to his master, Eli, thinking it was he who was calling him. Three times he did so until Eli realized it was the Lord trying to speak to Samuel. The next time God called, Samuel was ready and said to the Lord, "Speak, your servant is listening" (verse 10). From that time on, God began to reveal many things to Samuel. His stature grew in the eyes of the people and finally he became God's prophet to Israel. It all started with Samuel's attitude of attentiveness to what God had to say to him. He wanted to know what was on

the heart of God and God knew that Samuel would listen to what He had to say.

We need Samuel's attitude when we approach meditation.

Don Richardson tells the story of the Lisu Tribe in southern China. Tribal tradition taught about a white brother with a book of the true God written in the Lisu language. The members of the tribe were convinced of the story's veracity and waited anxiously for the white man with the book of God to come. When he finally did arrive, they embraced the book eagerly. The long awaited truth of God had arrived and tens of thousands of Lisu men and women gave their lives to the Lord.[2]

How much more should we, who have had the book of God all along, love the God who sent it to us and be eagerly listening to hear what He has to say to us from it?

David, as has already been pointed out, spent much time reading and meditating on the Word of God. During those times, God revealed many things to him, things about the state of David's heart and about the character of God's heart. In the process, David was changed. Godly character flowed from his life. So much so, that when his son, Absalom, led a rebellion against his rule and David was forced to flee Jerusalem, he reached out in forgiveness and reconciliation to his son, rather than in judgment and destruction. Indeed, he gave orders that Absalom was not to be killed in the ensuing battle. When he was killed, David mourned for him. They were the actions of a man who had heard from God. They were the actions of a man who had spent time with the Lord meditating on His Word.

Every meditator should have a heart desire for God as David had and the words of young Samuel upon their lips, "Speak, Lord, for your servant is listening." That is the attitude of a true Bible meditator.

Submission to God's Word

> I cleave to thy testimonies, O Lord; let me not be put
> to shame! (Psalm 119:31)

The psalmist says he cleaves to God's testimonies. Cleave is a word we do not use a lot today, so what does it mean? Basically it means to be stuck to something. Imagine someone spreading super-glue on their hands and then picking up an object, say a basketball. That is cleaving. They cleave to the basketball, they are stuck to it. Where they go, that ball goes. What they do, it does. It is there twenty-four hours a day stuck right to their hands. Now, because they have a basketball cleaving to their hands, the way they live their life has to change. They can not do all the things they used to do. Everything, the way they wash, the way they eat, even the way they sleep has to change to accommodate the ball. In a sense, they have to submit to the ball, it is right there with them always, and they have to adapt to it.

That is what the psalmist is saying. He is saying he is stuck to God's Word. It is as though he had picked up the Bible with his super-glued hands and it was there with him at every turn. His life had to change to accommodate God's Word. He had to submit to it.

As meditators, we must cleave to God's Word. We must submit to it and make room for it. The way we live our lives will have to change in the process. His Word must become precious to us, so precious that we want to be stuck to it at every turn. We want to be absorbed in His Word.

That is what it means to be in submission to God's Word.

Commitment to God's Word

It's true that to be submitted to God's Word implies that we must also be committed to it. Indeed, before we cleave to something, we must first be committed to it since it is going to become our constant companion. Nobody I know wants a constant companion with them to whom they are not committed.

Martin Luther was a man committed to the Word of God. He was willing to lay his neck on the line for God's Word. The church leadership of the day urged Luther to disavow his early writings regarding the plain teaching of Scripture. Knowing full well his response probably meant life or death, Luther stuck to his course. He stood and declared publicly to the authorities: "Since then your majesty and your lordships desire a simple reply, I will answer without horns and without teeth. Unless I am convicted by the Scriptures and plain reason—I do not accept the authority of popes and councils, for they have contradicted each other—my conscience is captive to the Word of God. God help me, Amen."[3]

God wants us to have the same unswerving commitment as Luther when we approach the Bible to meditate on it. The Scriptures promise that heaven and earth will pass away, but not God's Word. His Word is eternal and far outshines the importance of other temporal things. Luther knew this truth and weighed all his other commitments against the Word of God.

The psalmist also writes,

> I have laid up thy word in my heart, that I might not sin against thee. (Psalm 119:11)

So committed was the psalmist to God's Word that he wanted to store it up in his heart, not so he could prove to everyone how smart he was or how many Bible verses he could remember, but because he did not want to sin against God. He knew God's Word hidden away in his heart would keep his attention from any sin or wrong action with which he might be tempted.

How's our commitment to God's Word? Would we be able to stand and speak as Luther did if we were put to the test? Are we committed to God's Word like the psalmist was? Sometimes I am and sometimes I am not. When I'm not, I need to stop, pray and ask God to increase my commitment to His Word. That is the best thing to do when we feel our commitment to the Word of God waning.

While meditation is one of the ways we hide God's Word away in our hearts, we should also make reading large portions of Scripture to ourselves a regular habit. Are we able to recite the books of the Bible? Do we know the Ten Commandments? Do we know who Obadiah was or what he wrote? All of these things are important and we get to know them by regularly reading God's Word. The Bible is His eternal Word to us and we should make it our aim to get to know it.

Many of us look at the Bible and feel overawed by the amount of reading it presents us with. Did you know that someone with an average reading speed can read through the Bible in less than 100 hours? 100 hours to read all the eternal truth God has chosen to reveal to us. Some people spend nearly 100 hours a month just watching television. What eternal value does that hold?

Over the years, I have found it is good to read the Bible aloud to myself. I am sure many of you have had the experience of "reading" to the bottom of a page only to find you have no idea what you have just read. I have had that experience many times. Reading aloud to yourself can remedy this problem and help you remember more of what you have read. Educational psychologists have found that people remember about two or three times as much of what they read if they read it aloud. So read God's Word often and aloud.

Practice the Word of God

Thy testimonies are wonderful; therefore my soul keeps them. (Psalm 119:129)

Campbell McAlpine is a Scottish Bible teacher who has taught extensively on the topic of Bible meditation. For many years, he has meditated on the Word of God.

That meditation has shaped his ability to discern what God is saying to him and to obey what the Lord tells him.

According to McAlpine, a number of years ago, while he was living in Europe, he felt the Lord giving him some specific directions. He was to go to New Zealand and place a gospel of John in every home. Furthermore, the Lord told him he had one year in which to carry out the task and he was to ask no one for money or assistance in the venture. He was to solely trust the Lord.

Not only is New Zealand on the other side of the world from Europe, but there are about three million people living there, so this was no small task the Lord had called McAlpine to undertake.

Undaunted, he set out for New Zealand and after he arrived there, he was visited by a number of Christians. These people had been sovereignly led by God to come and bring up with McAlpine the issue of placing a gospel tract in every home in the nation. They offered their assistance, Campbell McAlpine accepted it and together they undertook the task. Amazingly, they completed the task one year to the day after McAlpine had received his instructions from God.

No one but God knows how many lives were impacted with His power as a result of receiving a gospel of John. However many it was, none of it would have been possible without the obedience of Campbell McAlpine. One man's obedience led to the release of God's power in the lives of many people in a nation on the other side of the world.

That is practicing the Word of God and it is what every Bible meditator must be prepared to do. To many this may sound frightening, but it's not. Campbell McAlpine is a mature and seasoned meditator on God's Word. What the

Lord asked him to do was, with God's help, within the scope of what McAlpine could accomplish. Certainly, Campbell McAlpine's faith was stretched by the task, but he was not humiliated by the task.

I have spoken with people over the years who have confessed to being scared to step out in obedience to the Lord. Many times as we have talked I have found that a negative view of God lay at the root of the problem. The person imagined that God would somehow bring their worst fears to bear upon them. Nothing is further from the truth. God always has our good in sight. There are times when he may want to stretch our faith a little, but He never wants to humiliate us. That is why Campbell McAlpine could step out and do what he did. He was confident that God had his good at heart and would not forsake him. As he stepped out, he proved God's character to be good and true.

Each of us can also rest in the goodness of God as we step out to obey Him and practice His Word.

The Proper Objects for Meditation

After we have fixed in our hearts the right attitude with which to approach meditating on the Word of God, we must then fix our hearts and minds on the right objects for meditation. There are four of these objects: the person of God, creation, the ways of God and the works of God.

The Person of God

> But the Lord is the true God; he is the living God and the everlasting King. At his wrath the earth quakes, and the nations cannot endure his

indignation....It is he who made the earth by his
power, who established the world by his wisdom,
and by his understanding stretched out the heavens.
When he utters his voice there is a tumult of waters
in the heavens, and he makes the mist rise from the
ends of the earth. He makes lightnings for the rain,
and he brings forth the wind from his storehouses.
(Jeremiah 10:10,12-13)

Contemplating such verses as these inspires awe in the
heart of the meditator. God is infinite and all powerful.
We can never know all that there is to know about Him, but
through focusing on the person of God we can catch
glimpses of who and what He is like- glimpses that will
strengthen our relationship with Him, glimpses that will
move our heart to love Him more, glimpses that will cause
us to lift up His name in praise, glimpses that will compel
us to seek Him more earnestly.

St. Maximus the Confessor was a seventh century
Greek monk who spent his life inquiring into the spiritual
truths of the Bible. Along the way, he made this pertinent
observation:

When the mind reflects on the absolute infinity of
God, on this unfathomable and greatly desirable
deep, it is first filled with wonder; and then it is
struck with amazement how God has brought into
being from nothing all that is. But as there is no end
to His greatness, so too is His wisdom unsearchable
(Ps.144:3). For how will he not be filled with
wonder, who contemplates this unapproachable
and awe-inspiring cause of goodness?[4]

If we want our faith to be made stronger, then we need

to meditate on the vastness of God; how infinite He is, and yet how interested this vast God is in the seemingly insignificant details of our daily lives. Such an observation will move our faith to new levels, as it did Joshua, David and many others down through the centuries who have inquired into the person of God.

Creation

Before I was a Christian, I remember climbing up 5,000 feet to the top of the Sandia Mountains east of my home in Albuquerque, New Mexico. This small group of mountains form part of the mighty Rocky Mountain range which stretches north from Mexico, through the United States, Canada and on into Alaska. As I stood on the top of those mountains, I was awe-struck by the amazing panorama spread out before me. I remember thinking, "There must be a God to create something so beautiful and breath-taking." It was a moment of revelation for me.

David had similar moments of revelation as he contemplated the wonders of creation. "The heavens declare the glory of God; the skies proclaim the work of his hands," he says in Psalms 19:1(NIV). At the end of this psalm, inspired by contemplating God's creation, he declares:

> May the words of my mouth and the meditation of
> my heart be pleasing in your sight, O Lord my Rock
> and my Redeemer. (verse 14, NIV).

Meditating on God's creation moved David to a response of personal devotion to the Lord.

The apostle Paul also recognized that through observing God's creation we could begin to learn about the creator. In Romans, he says:

> For since the creation of the world God's invisible qualities—his eternal power and divine nature— have been clearly seen, being understood from what has been made, so that men are without excuse (Romans 1:20, NIV).

How is it that we can contemplate God's creation and understand more about Him in the process? It is because the personality and being of the artist/creator is mirrored in His creation. What we see is a reflection of what God is like.

Perhaps you have had the joy of snorkeling along the edge of a coral reef. I used to live in Hawaii and had that pleasure on several occasions. When I did so, I was amazed by the seemingly infinite variety of aquatic life. There were fish of every imaginable shape, size and color. The coral itself was a brilliant display of differing shades and hues. Everywhere, underwater vegetation abounded. Why did God create all of those things? The Bible tells us He created them for His glory and pleasure. From observing a single coral reef, we can discern that God is a God of infinite variety. He pays close attention to the most meticulous details. He enjoys beauty and color. Because of all these things we can conclude that He is interested in His creation.

One of the greatest discoveries about the character of God was made by David after a time of meditating on creation. He posed his revelation in the form of a question to the Lord:

> What are human beings that you are mindful of
> them, mortals that you care for them?
> (Psalms 8:4, NRSV)

David had discovered the unique place human beings hold in God's creation. God truly cared for and wanted fellowship with humans. That, David had discovered, was why He made us.

Meditating on God's creation can reveal many other deep things to us about the character of the God we love and serve.

The Ways of God

> Now therefore, I pray thee, if I have found favor in
> thy sight, show me now thy ways, that I may know
> thee and find favor in thy sight... (Exodus 33:13)

This was Moses' cry to the Lord as he led Israel through the wilderness. He wanted to know God. God has done many great works, creation being one of them. His ways define why He does what He does. His ways are an expression of His character and personality. They are the motivation for His actions. That is what Moses asked God to reveal to him. Moses had already seen God perform amazing miracles in the course of delivering the Jews from the clutches of the Egyptians. Now he wanted to know what motivated those events. He wanted to see things from God's perspective.

Was Moses' request answered by the Lord?

David provides us with the answers:

> He made known his ways to Moses, his acts to the people of Israel. (Psalms 103:7)

Israel got to see the acts of God. Moses was allowed to view some of the motivations that caused God to act as He did.

David, too, sought to know the ways of God. Through many years of meditation, he began to glimpse the heart of God. Indeed, Psalms 103 is a meditation about the ways of God. The following is a sampling of just a few of the things David reveals about the ways of God:

> The Lord works vindication and justice for all who are oppressed. (verse 6)
> The Lord is merciful and gracious, slow to anger and abounding in steadfast love. (verse 8)
> He does not deal with us according to our sins, nor requite us according to our iniquities. (verse 10)
> As a father pities his children, so the Lord pities those who fear him. (verse 13)
> But the steadfast love of the Lord is from everlasting to everlasting upon those who fear him, and his righteousness to children's children. (verse 17)

The ways of God are an important object to focus on during times of meditation. Through meditating on the ways of God, we begin to discover interesting new insights about God; insights that strengthen our relationship with the Lord and enrich our daily lives.

The Works of God

> Make me understand the way of thy precepts, and
> I will meditate on thy wondrous works.
> (Psalms 119:27).

God has performed many amazing works. Many of these works are chronicled in the books of the Old and New Testaments. But of course, God is alive and active today; still doing many wondrous works in the world, in the church and in the lives of individual believers.

All of these works, David declares, are worthy objects for our meditation.

It's amazing, though, how quickly we can forget the deeds God has done for us. Psalms 78 tells how the children of Israel forgot the works that God had done on their behalf:

> They forgot what he had done, and the miracles that he had shown them. In the sight of their fathers he wrought marvels in the land of Egypt, in the fields of Zoan. He divided the sea and let them pass through it, and made the waters stand like a heap. In the daytime he led them with a cloud, and all the night with a fiery light. He cleft rocks in the wilderness, and gave them drink abundantly as from the deep. He made streams come out of the rock, and caused waters to flow down like rivers. (Psalms 78:11-16)

Can you imagine a million thirsty people wandering through the desert? Unable to find water anywhere, they cried out to God for help and supernaturally He caused enough water to satisfy their thirst to flow from a rock. Now this happened to Israel not once, but twice! Yet, somehow, they forgot the amazing miracles God performed for them and they fell into unbelief and sin. Meditating on the works of God reaffirms to our minds His awesome power.

However, meditating on the works of God not only reaffirms to us His power, but also the depth of His character. All of the works that God has performed down through the ages have been done for unworthy people. The things God has done in our lives, He has done not because we deserve them, but because He loves us. His works are an expression of that love to us. Continually, we need to ponder and consider the works of God and what they reveal to us about the greatness of God Himself.

So convinced of this was David, that as the book of Psalms begins drawing to a close, he again says:

> On the glorious splendor of thy majesty, and on thy
> wondrous works, I will meditate. (Psalm 145:5)

The Proper Effects of Meditation

Having brought the proper attitudes for meditation to bear upon the right objects for meditation, what are the effects this produces in our lives? Like attitudes and objects, there are four effects meditation has in our lives.

Meditating On God's Word Brings Conviction Of Sin

> I commune with my heart in the night; I meditate
> and search my spirit. (Psalms 77:6)

Meditation is a searching experience. During times of meditation, the Holy Spirit turns His searchlight on our lives. While it is proper to confess to God any known sin we have committed before we meditate, God will shine His light into the corners of our heart to convict us of any hidden sin that lurks there. Why does God do this? To make us better, more holy people? God's chief end and desire for man is to enjoy fellowship with Him. Sin destroys fellowship with God, so He does all He can to bring to our attention any unconfessed sin that is hiding in our hearts.

Times of Bible meditation cultivate our friendship with God. While the result of this cultivation is personal holiness, God's primary concern is for the health of our personal relationship with Him. Sin weakens that relationship, so God brings that sin to our attention.

Meditating on God's Word Gives Peace and Assurance

> Even though princes sit plotting against me, thy
> servant will meditate on thy statutes. (Psalm 119:23)

While we can not be exactly sure of all the circumstances that David was going through when he penned these words, we can make a reasonable guess. Tensions were mounting, a plan was afoot by some to dethrone David and take over the kingdom. So one of David's servants came to him and said, "Do you know what these people are saying about you and how they're plotting against you? What are you going to do about it?" David turned and asked another servant to bring him a copy of the law (the Scriptures). "I'll be elsewhere in the palace meditating on God's Word."

That was how David handled slander and plots against him. He meditated on God's Word. As he focused in on God and His lovingkindness and greatness, all David's fears were calmed. God was in control and in God, David would trust.

And that's how it should be for us today. As the circumstances of life assail us, we can find peace and assurance as we meditate on the Word of God. Our fears are calmed and the words recorded by the writer of the Proverbs come ringing to our ears, "Surely there is a future, and your hope will not be cut off" (Proverbs 23:18).

Meditating on God's Word Produces Greater Desire for Him and His Righteousness

Behold, I long for thy precepts; in thy righteousness give me life! (Psalm 119:40)

Think about your favorite food. Imagine you have not eaten that particular food in a while and a friend invites you over for a meal of it. Before you actually sit down to eat at your friend's house, you have imagined the meal. Your mind has replayed for you the aroma of the food cooking and in your mouth you can almost taste the succulent flavor.

That is what Bible meditation does for us. God's Word becomes food to our hearts and minds. We long for the times we spend with Him in His Word. We want to feed on it daily and absorb everything that His Word has to say to us so that we can become more like Him. If we go too long without feeding on His Word, if we are healthy, we begin to hunger and long for it.

Meditating on God's Word Gives Us Wisdom

Through meditating on God's Word, we can gain understanding as we begin to see God's perspective on things. While 1 Corinthians 13 teaches that our present understanding is incomplete and will not be perfected until we get to heaven, the Scriptures also testify to the fact that meditating on the Bible will provide us with more wisdom.

Well known Christian teacher, Bill Gothard, had been a mediocre student. At one point, he felt God show him about the need to memorize and meditate on Scripture. Almost from the day Gothard began to do this, his grades began improving, moving him near the top of his class.

A friend of mine, Danny Lehmann, reports that after years of using mind altering drugs he began to read, study and meditate on the Bible. Danny states that the power of God's Word restored his mind; today he has an international teaching and evangelistic ministry.

Meditating on God's Word brings intellectual health! Many high school drop outs, who have attended our Bible school, have found that their reading, thinking and study abilities improved markedly through spending time reading and meditating on the Bible.

All of this echoes the psalmist who said: "I have more understanding than all my teachers, for thy testimonies are my meditation" (Psalms 119:99). God truly will grant us wisdom and understanding when we meditate on His Word.

All of the steps, then, under attitudes, objects and effects contribute to the process of spiritual growth that occurs through meditation. Of course, the next most obvious question that arises is exactly how do we go about meditating on God's Word?

[1] *Charles H. Spurgeon*, W. Y. Fullerton, Moody Press, page 178.

[2] *Eternity in their Hearts*, Don Richardson, pages 73-102.

[3] *Christendom*, Roland Bainton, page 20-21

[4] Quoted in *The Nature and Character of God*, W. A. Pratney, page 65, Bethany House Publishers, Minneapolis, 1988.

Action Steps
Chapter Four

1. Describe your attitude toward God's Word to a friend. Do you love it? Do you feel relatively numb to it? Describe the way you feel about it.

2. Can you recite the 10 commandments. If so, write me and I will send you a free book.
Ron Smith
P.O.Box 3000
Lakeside, Montana 59922
USA

3. Have you read the whole Bible? Many people get stuck on the name lists and the kidneys in Leviticus. Skip them the first few times through the Bible. The name lists and the kidneys will wait for you. They will still be there your fourth time through the Bible.

4. Have you seen a miracle or a wonder? Describe it and talk to a friend about it. What was your emotional response to it? Did this change your relationship with God?

5. Is there any sin in your life? Have you

confessed it to Him and asked Him to cleanse you from it?

5

How to Meditate
on God's Word

As I rounded the corner on my way to teach a class one day, I came face to face with a cow. It was one of several cows who had wandered on to our training center property and who were nonchalantly chewing away on the lush green grass. The cow was completely absorbed with feeding and did not even flinch when we came eyeball to eyeball. Surprised at coming face to face with a cow, I watched it for a few moments. As I watched, I began to realize how much Bible meditation is like cows feeding! Cows bite off the grass and swallow it, but that is not the end of the digestive process for them. Later, they regurgitate the grass and chew on it some more. It is called chewing the cud. That is what Bible meditation is like- it is the spiritual equivalent of chewing the cud. It is taking small passages of Scripture and turning them over and over in our mind until we begin to unlock the truths God has stored in it for us.

At the beginning of the previous chapter, we saw how Spurgeon saw the Word of God as a rich Eldorado waiting to be discovered by each individual Christian. Well, our vehicle of discovery into that Eldorado is chewing the cud! We turn passages of God's Word over and over in our minds. We ask ourselves questions of it. We look at it from new angles, all with the ultimate intent of discovering the spiritual truth residing within. That is the true nature of Bible meditation.

In his biography of Francis Schaeffer, Louis Parkhurst has this to say about how Schaeffer meditated:

> Dr. Schaeffer read deeply and daily in the Bible. He strived to walk each day in prayerful practice of what the Bible taught. For these reasons, God gave him great insight into the Bible's teachings and how they relate to modern life. This does not mean Dr. Schaeffer's thoughts about the Bible and its answers to the problems of modern man came easily to him. He sometimes spent several years thinking through to the Bible's answer to a particular question. The answers he gave appeared to be effortless, and they were often repeated, but this was so because he had spent many days of prayer humbly seeking for the answers in the Word of God.[1]

This passage reveals clearly what chewing the cud, in the spiritual sense, is like. Francis Schaeffer took time—days, sometimes even years—to process passages of Scripture in search of their truth and spiritual significance to our daily lives. His efforts were rewarded and the church is the richer for the spiritual truths he unearthed.

In my own life, I have found the same to be true. On several occasions, I have spent more than six months meditating through a passage of Scripture. Indeed, I spent six months meditating on Psalms 119 and the truth that I unearthed revolutionized my whole meditation life.

There is no real pattern as to how and when a cow will chew his cud. When it's relaxed, when it has nothing better to do, when it needs more sustenance; they are all reasons why a cow decides to chew its cud when he does. But I can not pull my day-planner out and tell you that between 10:00 a.m. and 11:30 a.m. a particular cow will be chewing its cud. There is no formula to predict exactly how and when it will decide to do so. It's that way with Bible meditation, too. Bible meditation is not formula oriented. The point of the process is to get the maximum spiritual goodness from God's Word.

Meditating on the Bible is a very personal activity and as such should suit our personality. Some will want to add a certain amount of structure to their meditation times, others will not. Some may find it more advantageous to meditate in the morning, while others may find evenings or some other part of the day to be better. What is important is not that we all follow the same procedure, but that we establish a pattern of meditating that assures we get the maximum spiritual benefit in our lives.

With this in mind, the following points are simply guides, not laws, on how to effectively meditate. Take them and adapt them to your needs.

STEPS TO EFFECTIVE BIBLE MEDITATION

**Step One: Choose a Quiet and Interruption-
Free Time and Place in which to Meditate**

Many significant leaders throughout history have emphasized the importance of finding a place and time to quiet themselves before the Lord.

In Psalms 119:62, David talks about rising at midnight to praise and be with the Lord. I imagine, as King of Israel, that was when he knew he was not going to be interrupted.

Jesus found it necessary to go off by Himself to a "lonely place" where He could commune with His Father free from the interruptions of people. Sometimes, He would rise early in the morning and do so; while, at other times, he would go there after a period of ministry.

John Wesley made it a habit to rise early, usually about 4:30 a.m., so he could spend uninterrupted time fellowshipping with the Lord.

Dr. Harold Ockenga, founder of both Fuller Seminary and Gordon-Conwell Theological Seminary, had one particular corner in a special room of his house where he would meditate on and read God's Word each day.

Of course, in our urban world, it is not always that easy to find a place away from others and free from interruptions. Jackie Pullinger works among drug addicts in Hong Kong, in a part of the city that is considered one of the world's most densely populated areas. She tells how difficult it is, especially for new workers coming from overseas to work with her, to find a quiet place where they can practice effective Bible meditation. I lived in Hong Kong for a time and can attest to how busy and crowded the city is. Yet even there, it is possible to enjoy fulfilling times of meditating on God's Word. It may take a little more planning on our part, but it certainly is not impossible. Sometimes the only place of refuge may be the quiet place within. Perhaps as we ride the bus or other public transport to work or school, we can mentally withdraw into our inner sanctum where we can be alone with God. But as a general rule, it is best to find a physical place that is quiet and free from interruptions.

Archibald Hart, Dean and Professor of Psychology at Fuller Theological Seminary, lists some practical things to do before beginning a period of Bible meditation. He says:

> Ensure you won't be interrupted. Lock the door, hang out a sign, tell spouse, kids, and neighbors not to disturb you or go where they can't find you. Unplug the telephone and make sure the stove is off.[2]

For some, just the thought of withdrawing for a period of time each day sends chills down their spine. In our hectic paced world some find that even if they want to, they just can not seem to relax and slow down. They are driven to be always busy and Bible meditation somehow does not fit the busy mold for them. Archibald Hart identifies these people as adrenalin addicts and lists a number of symptoms by which this addiction can be identified. These symptoms include:

> 1) A strong compulsion to be "doing something" while at home or on vacation.

2) An obsession with thoughts about "what was left undone."
3) A feeling of vague guilt while resting.
4) Fidgetiness, restlessness, pacing, leg kicking.
5) An inability to concentrate for very long on any relaxing activity.
6) Feelings of irritability and aggravation.
7) A vague (or sometimes profound) feeling of depression whenever you stop an activity.[3]

This is not a book on recovery from addiction. These symptoms are only mentioned because I am surprised, as I travel the country and share on the topic of Bible meditation, how many people confess to being troubled by some or all of these symptoms. If you recognize yourself in them, then establishing a regular time of meditation is going to feel like climbing a mountain, but keep moving forward. Ask God for His strength as you do so. Be assured, the benefits you receive in your life from a regular time of Bible meditation will far outweigh the struggle that it takes you to establish such a habit.

So, the first step along the way to practicing effective Bible meditation is to find a quiet place where you will not be interrupted. For some this may be a bedroom, a closet, the living room or perhaps an office. Where you choose to meditate is not as important as the fact that it is a quiet, interruption-free place. For me, that place is a big easy chair in my study to which I retreat each morning and many evenings. It is where I kick back, relax and meditate on a small portion of Scripture.

Find your place for meditation and make it your sanctuary.

Step Two: Pray and Ask God to Show You on Which Passage of Scripture He Wants You to Begin Meditating.

The successful meditator chews daily on small portions of Scripture. It's not best or even possible to thoroughly meditate on large passages of God's Word. Instead, we should concentrate our energies on small, bite-size portions which we can chew on all day.

For those who are new to Bible meditation, it is essential that you begin in the right place. Some parts of Scripture are more conducive than others to meditation. It's probably not best to begin meditating in Leviticus, although God could direct some people to it. That is not to say there is nothing of spiritual value in Leviticus. Leviticus is a rich storehouse of truth about God. However, it is a long and sometimes difficult book to read and understand, which means it is not really a good place to start your journey into Bible meditation.

Below are a few suggestions of some good places to start your meditation. God alone knows which part of His Word will be of most use to you, so pray and ask Him where He wants you to begin meditating on His Word.

Psalms 119

This psalm emphasizes the beauty of God's Word. In it, David pours out his heart as he shows the supreme place the Word of God should have in our lives.

As I mentioned earlier, I spent six months meditating through this psalm a verse at a time. In that six months my love for, delight in, and understanding of God's Word grew tremendously.

The Ten Commandments (Exodus 20:1-17)

Meditating on the Ten Commandments gives us fresh insight into the nature and character of God. We begin to see more clearly the things God loves and the things He hates. Such insight will, in turn, help us to shape the way we live so that it will be pleasing to the Lord.

The Sermon on the Mount (Matthew 5-7)

The value of meditating through these chapters is to see the importance that Jesus places on our actions, as well as, our responses to people and situations. These portions of Scripture can provide the basis for a fruitful period of meditation on the growth and development of Christian character.

1 Corinthians 13

This is Paul's great chapter on love. The reasons for wanting to make it a starting point for our meditation are obvious, as are the benefits that will accrue in our lives as a result.

The Book of Proverbs

This book is a gold mine of wisdom for every follower of the Lord. In it, Solomon shares deep and abiding truths, truths that we can apply to our everyday living.

It is a good practice to meditate through whole books

of the Bible, beginning with Chapter 1, verse 1 and going through to the end. During the weeks and months of meditating on the book, it is also wise to read a book through a number of times to get the context for daily meditations.

Whatever passage of Scripture the Lord leads you to, remember to take it in bite-sized pieces. That may mean meditating on a few words, a phrase, a verse or perhaps even a couple of verses a day. What is important is that you fully digest what you take in. Remember, meditating is not about formulas- it is about digesting the Word of Truth. So meditate on digestible portions.

Step Three: Think Through the Selected Passage Again and Again—Prayerfully

Having chosen a passage of Scripture, the next thing to do is to focus in on it and think it through. This is the time where God begins to give us insight into the truths encapsulated within the verses we are meditating on.

Missionary statesman, David Ross, has this to say on the subject:

> "As we meditate, we clear our minds of all unclean or unnecessary thoughts, or all distractions, in order to focus our minds on the Word before us. When we meditate, we allow the Holy Spirit to direct our spirits, like a rudder guides a boat, to the goal of the Word we are meditating on.
>
> Rabbi David Kimchi sees meditation as embracing the Word in much the same way a woman would embrace a diamond, caressing it, gazing upon it, pondering over it and reflecting

upon it until we begin to see and discover the many new facets of light and color, the new revelations of God and His truth....

To focus on the Word is to ponder the Word and store it in our hearts (not just in our minds) as Mary did (Luke 2:19). The Word then will never leave us!

To focus on the Word is to set our minds on the Word, on God's truth, to concentrate on Him and what He desires to say, to fix our gaze upon Him and concentrate with our minds and hearts."[4]

The following points will help us to properly focus our thoughts on God's Word.

Read

Read the passage of Scripture you are meditating on slowly and prayerfully to yourself 10-15 times. I find it helps if I read it aloud to myself. The point is to become totally familiar with what is contained in the passage. Make a mental note of any words that stand out as you read.

Question

After you have thoroughly familiarized yourself with what is contained in the passage, ask yourself some questions about the passage.

- What was the geography like where the events occurred?
- Who is involved and what are they doing?
- Why are they doing what they are doing?
- What would it have been like to be there as the events unfolded? What would I have seen, heard, smelled or

thought if I had been there? Use your imagination. It is amazing how the stories of Scripture come alive when we try to place ourselves there at the time the events are unfolding. We begin to notice things that we have not noticed before. Our eyes are opened to see kernels of truth that we have glossed over in past readings of the passage.

Consider

Having read and asked questions of the passage, it is time to consider more closely the various aspects of it.

Howard Hendricks lists eight points to consider when thinking about a passage of Scripture in order to see how it applies to our lives.

"• Is there an example to follow?
• Is there a sin to avoid?
• Is there a promise to claim?
• Is there a prayer to repeat?
• Is there a command to obey?
• Is there a condition to meet?
• Is there an error to mark?
• Is there a challenge to face?"[5]

As well, we should also consider:

• Are there things about the people in the passage that I should imitate in my life?

• Do their lives reveal traits that God is not pleased with and which I know I have?

• Are there other things in the passage which I should be doing?

• Are there any miracles that occur in the passage? Am I asking God to do similar things in my life?

• Are there any other things God may be saying to me through the passage?

Of course, there are times when we may do all of this and God does not seem to show us anything. Do not worry. All has not been in vain. Several days later, you may encounter a situation and, suddenly, the treasure of the passage you were meditating on hits you. You can see how it relates to the situation you are facing. That has been my experience on more than one occasion. So relax and enjoy your time of meditation. No one is going to test you at the end of twenty minutes to see how much truth God has revealed to you.

Ordinarily, a time of Bible meditation should last for about 15 to 20 minutes. When you finish your period of meditating, do not just leave things there. Call the passage to mind throughout the day. Continue to turn it over in your thoughts as you work or play. Remember, meditation is like a cow chewing its cud, and cows do that throughout the day. If you like, the time we spend meditating is like feeding time. It is when we ingest God's Word in such a way that we can come back and chew on it some more to derive further goodness from it throughout the day. Sometimes, I like to repeat the verse out loud to myself during the day. Often, I simply reflect on what I meditated on earlier in the morning. Not only does this help me to remember the passage, it also helps me focus in on it again.

A single sentence of Scripture can change our life. Remember Lazarus, Jesus said only three words to him, "Lazarus come forth!" With that, a dead man was raised back to life. Or Augustine, reading one passage of Scripture was enough to convince him he needed to be converted.

Remember, God's Word is powerful and when we center in on the truth of it, through the agency of the Holy Spirit, God releases His power into our lives. Power to make us a little more like Him each day. Power to live a righteous, upright life.

A word of warning from Martin Luther is appropriate before moving to the next step in meditation

> Take care you do not grow weary or think you have done enough when you have read, heard, and spoken them (verses of Scripture) once or twice, and you then have complete understanding.[6]

Keep on reading, questioning and considering the Word of God!

Step Four: Apply the Word

The goal of meditation is to know God more intimately and to obey Him more closely. Everything else we derive from meditating is a side benefit. 1 John 1:7 tells us that in order to walk in close fellowship with God, we must walk in the light. What does it mean to walk in the light? 1 John 1:6 gives context and more understanding:

> If we say we have fellowship with him while we walk in darkness, we lie and do not live according to the truth. (1 John 1:6)

If to walk in darkness means not living according to the truth, then to walk in the light is to live according to the truth.

Meditation is a quest to discover the spiritual truths of God's Word. However, those truths are worthless to us unless we apply them to our lives. So after thinking through and chewing on the verse we have been meditating upon, we must apply the truths we discover.

This may involve confessing and repenting of some hidden sin that God brings to our attention. It may mean dealing with some habit we have or working to repair a broken or damaged relationship. Perhaps God may require us to deal with our attitude toward money and material possessions by donating some of our money to our church, a ministry or by giving some of our things to the poor.

The possibilities are endless. What is important is that we follow through in applying God's Word to our lives.

Often applying the Word takes time as we work through situations. Sometimes it may not be easy, but if we ask God, He will give us the strength to carry on until that area of our life is brought into submission to His will and Word.

There are times when meditating on God's Word will pump us up spiritually for the day and there are other times, such as when God reveals areas of our life that need to be brought into line with His Word, when we will feel deflated, even defeated. But the fact that the Creator of the Universe has taken the time to reveal that area to us is a mark of just how much He cares for us. He is not prepared to settle for a second-best relationship with us. He wants the best! He has brought that situation to our attention because it is a roadblock to that best relationship.

Eating health food is not that exhilarating to the taste buds. I have used a health drink called barley grass at times throughout the years. I certainly do not drink it for the flavor! (My wife describes it as "drinking the bottom of a lake.") Nonetheless, I know my body will benefit from that drink in the long run, so I keep drinking.

That is the perspective we need as we daily apply God's truth in our life. If we continually apply His Word, it will do us good.

Of course, applying God's Word in our life does not always mean dealing with large personal issues, sometimes it involves the mundane. Several years ago, I was meditating on a verse in Deuteronomy 24. The verse spoke about not oppressing a hired servant, but giving him the wages he deserves and has earned. As I pondered through the verse, the Lord really showed me some principles in regard to tipping. I began trying to leave the tip on the table in cash rather than putting it on my credit card. Sometimes, the server has to wait a whole month before he gets his tip if it is charged on a credit card, but if it is left in cash on the table, he gets what is due him immediately.

God may show you truths that relate to some fairly ordinary issues as you meditate on His Word. But no matter how mundane, apply His truth to your life.

Step Five: Relax and Enjoy The Lord

In the 17th century, an assembly in England composed the *Westminster Confession of Faith*. When a person joins the Presbyterian church, they are often asked a question from that confession: What is the chief end of man? The correct answer is: "to glorify God and enjoy Him forever."

To glorify God in our bodies is an injunction from New Testament theology. However, we can not properly enjoy God and glorify Him if we never stop to rest and relax in the Lord.

Jesus recognized this. After times of hectic ministry, He would withdraw so He could relax and commune with His Father. If the Son of God needed to do that, how much more so do we?

One passage in the Old Testament records a man being stoned to death for failing to rest as prescribed by God in the law. Most of us today, though, do not need to be stoned for failing to rest and relax, since our failure to relax is slowly killing us anyway! All manner of physical ailments from high blood pressure, to heart disease, to possible increased risk of cancer, have been shown in studies to have a possible link to people who regularly overwork and over-stress themselves. The best counter for such a situation is for people to slow down, relax and enjoy the things around them.

Regarding relaxing, Archibald Hart writes:

> Relaxation should be an hourly, daily, and weekly event.
> *Hourly,* we should be checking up on our tensions and saying "relax" to ourselves. I would suggest placing a small colored piece of paper or some other kind of mark on your mirror, watch dial, steering wheel, pen, or glasses to remind you to do this.
> *Daily,* you should spend at least thirty minutes in deep relaxation. This is such a small part of the

> day that everyone can afford to take it—and none
> of us can afford not to. The best time is when you
> come home from work or when your early evening
> duties are completed. Parents of small children
> may find the best time is right after the children are
> put to bed.
> *Weekly,* there needs to be a longer period of
> relaxation. Sundays or Sabbaths are ideal. On
> these days, cut back on work activities. Take time
> to put your feet up, have a nap, or just be lazy.[7]

Chapter seven lays out a number of other helpful points on how to have a time of effective relaxation and Bible meditation.

One thing I have noticed is that when I am relaxed, I tend to notice things I had not seen before. Little things, unimportant things, but things that help me understand better the situations going on around me and why I react to them in certain ways.

Effective Bible meditation often consists of noticing the little things, noticing the little things can open new vistas of spiritual truth to us.

So make relaxing and enjoying the Lord an important part of your daily practice of Bible meditation.

Some Words of Advice

Note has already been made of the fact that our goal for meditation should be to meditate on the Word of God from 15-20 minutes, and that we should strive to make this a daily habit. This is only a guide, not a law. I try to meditate for 15 to 30 minutes each morning and then, if possible, in the evening after I have climbed into bed I try to center my thoughts on the verse from my morning meditation time to meditate some more on it. Your personality, however, may be quite different from mine, so devise a meditation schedule that suits you.

Remember also, meditation is not spiritual fast food, but something that nourishes our lives through constant practice. I have met many who have decided to make Bible meditation a part of their life only to drop it after two or three weeks because they felt the results were not dramatic enough. Remember, a strong, succulent and fruitful tree does not just grow overnight. It takes a sustained period (often several years) of incremental growth to get to that stage. So make Bible meditation a regular habit.

Of course, to make something a regular habit requires some commitment and discipline on our part. We may need to restructure our schedule to allow for a daily period of meditation. We may have to re-evaluate some of our priorities. But if we stick to it, our time meditating on God's Word will become one of the foundation stones in our relationship with the Lord. As our relationship with Him grows, our meditation time will become so important that we will guard it vigorously to keep it free of interruptions so that we can derive maximum spiritual benefit in our lives.

[1] *Francis Schaeffer, The Man and His Message*, Louis Parkhurst, p. 18

[2] *Adrenalin and Stress*, Archibald Hart, Word Books, p. 172.

98

[3] *Adrenalin and Stress*, Hart, p. 89.

[4] *The Church's Lost Treasure*, David Ross.

[5] *Living by the Book*, Howard Hendricks, Moody Press p. 308.

[6] *Luther's Works*, Vol. 34, quoted in Christianity Today, Oct. 4,'93

[7] *Adrenalin and Stress*, Hart, p. 148.

How to Meditate

**Step 1: Choose a quiet place
and interruption-free
time in which to meditate.**

**Step 2: Pray and ask God to
show you which passage of
Scripture he wants you to begin
meditating on.**

**Step 3: Think through the selected
passage again and again—
prayerfully.**

Step 4: Apply the Word.

**Step 5: Relax and enjoy the
Lord.**

6

Words into Action

It is easy to get theoretical when discussing any spiritual discipline and meditation is no exception. The point of this chapter, though, is to try and be as practical as possible; to put the words of the previous chapter into action. To do this, I have drawn on several meditations from my personal experience.

These meditations are shared in an attempt to walk you through the process of Bible meditation, showing how the steps illuminated in chapter five flow naturally together. They are not shared for you to follow as an exact pattern of how you should meditate. Meditation is an intensely personal endeavor. Therefore, develop your own pattern for meditating. By all means, draw upon my approach, but do not follow it as law. Adapt my approach to meditation to your own needs and style.

The meditations contained in this chapter are offered as examples that will lead you into a daily habit of Bible meditation.

Meditation One

> He divided the sea and let them pass through it and
> made the waters stand like a heap. (Psalms 78:13)

I had been meditating through Psalms 78, a verse at a time. The psalm describes God's powerful work in the history of Israel, referring to many of the signs and wonders God performed in delivering the Jews from Egypt.

I slumped into my easy chair and read the verse through to myself a number of times. As I read it through, I began to wonder what water standing in a heap would actually look like. I thought about how it would have looked to a five year old boy as he walked through the Red Sea. I began to imagine myself looking through that boy's eyes. As he looked down at his feet, they were planted firmly on sand, but sand that was usually buried at the bottom of the sea under several feet of water. As the boy looked to the left and to the right, there was the water that usually covered the sand standing "like a heap." It looked like clear jello, wobbling, swaying, pulsating, but staying put so the Children of Israel could cross the Red Sea on dry land.

Then the small boy looked behind him and there were the feared Egyptian soldiers. An interesting thing was happening, the water was crashing down on them like an avalanche. Men in their military armor struggled to get to the surface as chariots, horses and soldiers were swept away by the crashing tons of water.

It was a miraculous event God performed that day.

That young boy would never doubt God's ability to miraculously watch over him.

But what about me? Did I have the same confidence as that small boy? Did I truly believe God could do miracles in my life? Did I really think God would or could deliver me from seemingly hopeless situations?

I began to pray and ask the Lord to give me the unswerving faith in His miraculous ability to deliver me, which that small boy must have had.

Over the years, I have come back to this meditation. Today, it still continues to feed and challenge me in my relationship with the Lord.

Meditation Two

> Make me understand the way of thy precepts, and
> I will meditate on thy wondrous works.
> (Psalm 119:27)

I sat down beside beautiful Flathead Lake, a short walk from my home in Montana, to meditate on this verse. I sat looking across the lake at the Mission Mountains which rise up from the other side of the lake. I was taken aback by the grandeur of the sight. I began counting the mountain peaks I could see in this small part of God's creation; there were over eighty of them.

I took the advice of the verse I was meditating on and began to center my thoughts on the wondrous works of God laid out before me. I began to think of the power of the spoken Word of God who by His Word created all things in heaven and on the earth. I thought about the power of Jesus who is the Word of God and the fact that everything was made through Him. The gospel of John states that "all things were made through Him."

I began to pray and ask God to give me greater faith in His powerful Word. If His Word was strong enough to create the majestic mountains before me, then it was also strong enough to do amazing wonders in my life.

Meditation Three

In November of 1985, I meditated through 1 Samuel 24. At that time, I was on a ministry trip through the South Pacific Islands of Samoa, Fiji and Tonga. On one particular day, I sat on a beach in Pago Pago, Samoa, to do my meditating. The beautiful blue Pacific lapped at the glistening white sand and fishermen fished from the rocks at one end of the beach.

In 1 Samuel, King Saul placed David over the army of Israel, he even married his daughter off to him, but Saul became enraged by David's success. He was eaten up with jealousy, he threw spears at his young general and stalked him through the wilderness. Finally, in a cave where Saul slept, David's chance came to kill him, but David refused to give in to the temptation and the prodding of his fellow soldiers to kill Saul. Instead, he cut off the corner of Saul's robe. Afterward David and Saul are both outside the cave and David calls to the crazy King Saul:

> Lo, this day your eyes have seen how the Lord gave you today into my hand in the cave; and some bade me kill you, but I spared you. I said, "I will not put forth my hand against my lord; for he is the Lord's anointed." (1 Samuel 24:10)

I traveled on to Fiji and God began to bring back to my mind the earlier meditation in Samoa.

At the time, I was finishing doctoral studies in theology, with only my thesis remaining to be written. As I thought more about the verse, the Lord began to show me how it was related to my thesis. He began to show me that I had a proud attitude about my studies. "You want to kill him don't you?" The Lord spoke into my mind. At first I thought it related to the verse, few of us could have been as restrained as David. We would have wanted to kill Saul then and there. The Lord directed my thoughts beyond, to the man I was attacking in my thesis. I soon saw that in my pride, I was willing to hurt a man and his reputation over a point of theology. I wanted to exalt myself and show that I was right and he was wrong. Not only was I going to prove it, I was going to receive a doctorate for proving it.

On that day in Fiji, I was humbled before the Lord. I began to weep and confess my sin to Him. Then the Lord showed me that I also needed to confess my sin to several other people. It was not easy to do, but it was worth it. I arrived back in the United States from my trip a changed man.

That time on a beach in the South Pacific, meditating on God's Word and applying its message to my life was a turning point in my ministry.

Meditation Four

...A man is not justified by works of the law but through faith in Jesus Christ, even we have believed in Christ Jesus, in order to be justified by faith in Christ, and not by works of the law, because by

works of the law shall no one be justified.
(Galatians 2:16)

I was thousands of miles from home, sitting on the lawn of a missionary's home in Seoul, Korea, meditating on the doctrine of justification.

The word "justification" comes from the Greek legal system. God justifies sinners, declaring them to be righteous by His grace. I had preached on the topic of God's grace on numerous occasions.

But the longer I sat on that lawn meditating on Galatians 2:16, the more convinced I became that I was a legalist in certain areas of my life. The Lord began to show me that although I preached grace, I lived some grace and some law.

Unfortunately, I also saw that some of the disciples I had made were legalistic as well. It showed itself in many ways. They scorned anyone who missed church or who did not constantly witness or tithe.

I was devastated. God pulled away the mask I had been living behind. I saw that I had been trying to gain false favor from God through being legalistic, while all the while He had wanted me to stop striving, relax and enjoy His righteousness in my life.

There and then I prayed and determined before the Lord that I would make grace a central theme in my life. From that time it has been so. I wrote a graduate thesis on the topic and published a book on Galatians titled, *Grace Simply Grace.*

Meditation Five

For God alone my soul waits in silence; from him
comes my salvation. (Psalms 62:1)

In the refuge of my easy chair, I meditated through
this verse. As I read it out loud to myself several times,
the two words "God alone" seemed to stand out to me. I
pondered over the words and, as I did so, I began to see that
there are times when we face situations about which we
are powerless to do anything. God alone is our only source
of help and hope.

This message impacted my life greatly several weeks
later as I headed to what I thought would be my mother's
funeral. Several days earlier, my mom had undergone
surgery and, at first, she seemed to be recovering well.
Then things took a turn for the worst and she had to have
a second round of surgery. During that surgery her blood
pressure dropped dramatically, her heart began beating
over 190 times per minute and her temperature shot up to
107° F.

As I flew home to what seemed to be a hopeless
situation for my mom, I was reminded of my meditation
on "God alone" being the source of our help and hope.
There on the airplane I prayed and released the situation to
the Lord, acknowledging as I did so that there was nothing
I could do to help the situation, that it was in His hands—
He alone was the only one who could deal with the
situation.

To my amazement, and God's glory, my mother did not die. God saw fit to heal her.

I trust that these sample meditations have been helpful in allowing you to see the different ways the process of Bible meditation works. I also trust that you are challenged to make Bible meditation a regular part of your life.

While the immediate benefit of this type of meditation is spiritual, leading to an enhanced relationship with the Lord, there are also other benefits that come from following a regular habit of meditation.

---

1. Make a lifetime commitment to meditate, understanding that you will miss a day or two here and there.

2. Remember that Bible meditation is spiritual warfare. If the enemy attacks you in this, ask someone to pray for you.

3. If you miss a day, make a decision early on to pick it up and persevere. The victory in meditation comes through endurance and perseverance.

4. Ten or twenty minutes a day is a do-able goal.

How to Meditate

Step 1: Choose a quiet place and interruption-free time in which to meditate.

Step 2: Pray and ask God to show you which passage of Scripture he wants you to begin meditating on.

Step 3: Think through the selected passage again and again—prayerfully.

Step 4: Apply the Word.

Step 5: Relax and enjoy the Lord.

7

Other Benefits

God's Word is powerful! Chapter one of this book is a declaration of this truth. Reading, meditating on and studying God's Word allows the power of God to be released into our lives. The physiological mechanics involved in meditating on God's Word also have a beneficial effect on us. Thus, the practice of meditation combined with the power of God's Word can produce lasting spiritual, physical and psychological benefits.

A number of eminent researchers have studied and documented the physiological benefits of meditating. Indeed, there have been more than 400 articles written by various doctors concerning the medical benefits of meditation. This research is focused on both meditating in general. This chapter is a chronicling of some of the findings.

Dr. Herbert Benson, Associate Professor of Medicine at Harvard, has spent twenty years studying the benefits of meditation, and has published his findings in a book titled, *The Relaxation Response*. While Benson's book is written from a scientific/research perspective not from a Christian point of view, he mentions Pastor John Wimber among others.

In his book, Benson says that a Christian meditating on Scripture can (though it does not always happen) break such anxiety related symptoms as nausea, vomiting, diarrhea and constipation. The meditator can also break short-temperedness, combat attacks of hypertension, alleviate such pains as headaches and backaches, effectively treat hypertension, deal with some heartbeat irregularities and alleviate insomnia.

Meditation can also be utilized in the treatment of cancer, helping patients deal more effectively with their unfortunate situation.

For any Christian wanting to begin meditating on the Scriptures, Benson recommends the Psalms as a good place to start.

In *Beyond the Relaxation Response* (the sequel to *The Relaxation Response*), Benson writes that some people are healed through meditation. The steps to healing are usually gradual and follow a certain path. First, the patient becomes less concerned about the symptoms or illness and their anxiety cycle is broken. Second, the symptoms become less severe. Third, the symptoms are present less of the time and short periods of complete relief are noted in the patient. Fourth, the periods of relief become longer. And fifth, the symptoms are either completely gone or remain in a fashion that no longer interferes with everyday activities.

Benson states in his book:

In fact, I've found that many patients have difficulty in remembering their original symptoms....

The time duration for a person to experience these full benefits is quite variable, for some it can be as short as 1 or 2 weeks, for others up to a year is required. Most people can expect improvements to occur in 4 to 6 weeks.[1]

Dr. Benson also states that meditation enhances creativity. There has been a Christian study done on this aspect of creativity as well. Dr. Archibald Hart, Dean of the School of Psychology at Fuller Theological Seminary, writes in his book, *Adrenalin and Stress:*

Contrary to what many people believe, it is when we are minimally aroused by adrenalin that we can do our most innovative and imaginative thinking.[2]

Such relaxation, according to Hart, can be achieved through meditation. As we relax and relish the Word, God can make us more creative.

Hart also writes in *Adrenalin and Stress:*

What is unfortunate is that we as Christians have not shown the world as clearly as we ought that the practice of genuine Christianity can more effectively reduce stress and help people live more fulfilling lives. We are often so frantic in living out our faith that we cause more stress than we cure. This should become a challenge for us, particularly as we develop our prayer lives and rediscover that there is a Christian meditation—too long neglected by twentieth-century Christians—that can produce profound peace and communication with God. Perhaps we will then be able to share the experience of the psalmist, who said, "Mark this well, the Lord has set apart the redeemed for himself. Therefore he will listen to me and answer when I call to him. Stand before the Lord in awe, and do not sin against him. Lie quietly upon your bed in silent meditation" (Psalms 4:3-4 LB).[3]

Dr. Hart then goes on to discuss the basic ingredients of all relaxation. His insights are pertinent and I quote him at length.

There is nothing mysterious or mystical about relaxation. It is a natural response of the body and can be triggered by all of us. In and of itself it does not have spiritual significance, but as we shall see, it can be combined with prayer and Christian meditation to produce a powerful spiritual exercise. It is something that becomes easier as you practice it.

Whatever body system you are trying to relax, the following are the basic steps to relaxation:

1. Sit or lie in a comfortable position. Pain or pressure will keep you in an aroused state, so try to minimize discomfort. Loosen tight clothing and remove your glasses. Try to provide support for all the undersides of your body.

2. Ensure that you won't be interrupted. Lock the door; hang out a sign; tell spouse kids, and neighbors not to disturb you, or go to where they can't find you. Unplug the telephone and make sure the stove is off.

3. Set aside a predetermined amount of time (say, thirty or forty-five minutes) for the exercise. Set an alarm so you won't have to keep checking on

the time.
 4. Don't fall asleep. If you need sleep, go ahead
and sleep, but don't confuse this with "relaxing".
Relaxation is a conscious experience not a trance or
sleeplike state. If you fall asleep when relaxing,
you probably need more sleep.
 5. Remain inactive. Don't fidget, move, get up,
or scratch. At first you'll want to do all this because
you will be experiencing withdrawal symptoms
from the effect of lowering your adrenalin, just as
occurs when you stop taking a powerful drug. Just
put up with the discomfort and it will pass away. (If
the need to scratch becomes unbearable, then go
ahead, but return as quickly as possible to the
relaxed position.)
 6. Avoid thinking troublesome thoughts. Set
aside your worries. Pray and "let him have all your
worries and cares, for he is always thinking about
you and watching everything that concerns you"
(1 Peter 5:7, LB). Try to detach yourself from your
worrisome world for a while and remain free of the
demands that press on you.[4]

Hart's research into the benefits of meditation also
found that cholesterol levels have been reduced by reducing
adrenal secretion. Recent studies have shown that high
cholesterol levels are related to our diet and to increased
adrenalin levels in our bodies. Meditation cuts down the
amount of adrenalin that our body secretes. So, as a person
continues to meditate, it is possible that he can reduce his
cholesterol level.
 Dr. Dean Ornish, Clinical Fellow of Medicine at
Harvard, documented some of the work of Benson and
others. He concluded:

114

> The physiological effects...produced by meditation are beneficial to people with coronary heart disease....
>
> Since meditation may reduce the frequency of irregular heart beats, it may reduce the frequency of sudden death due to ventricular fribillation in heart attacks, though this has not yet been proven.[5]

From my own experience, I can testify to the fact that my energy level throughout the day seemed to rise significantly after two or three months of meditating.

Dr. Paul Meier, of the Minirth-Meier Clinic in Dallas, Texas, himself a regular meditator on the Word of God, studied several hundred candidates for the ministry at a Midwestern seminary. Meier surveyed the student body and divided them into three categories. The first group included those who meditated daily on the Word of God and had done so for the previous three years or more. The second group was made up of those who meditated daily on the Word and had done so for the previous three months. The third group consisted of those who had never meditated on the Word of God. Dr. Meier's goal in the study was to determine how stable these students were emotionally and psychologically.

Meier's conclusions were as he had expected. The least stable group were those who never meditated. Those who were relatively stable had meditated daily for at least the past three months. The most stable students were those who had meditated daily and had done so for three years or more. Dr. Meier documented his study in the book, *Meditating For Success*.

Meditation is good for us. When that meditation is focused on the Word of God, it nourishes us spiritually, physically and psychologically.

Of course, none of this should be a surprise to us. It was, after all, the writer of the Proverbs who, all those hundreds of years ago, wrote:

> Keep these thoughts ever in mind; let them penetrate deep within your heart, for they will mean real life for you, and radiant health.
> (Proverbs 4:21-22, LB)

[1] *Beyond the Relaxation Response*, Herbert Benson, page 121.

[2] *Adrenalin and Stress*, Archibald Hart, page 178.

[3] *Ibid*, page 150.

[4] *Ibid*, page 151.

[5] *Stress, Diet and Your Heart*, Dean Ornish, page 348.

Conclusion

On a recent flight I was seated next to a woman in her late 30's. The woman was busy reading a book called, *The Seven Steps of Zen*. As she read along, she would scratch down notes in the book margins and on a separate sheet of paper. I was impressed with her diligence, nothing seemed to interrupt her concentration.

Finally, she stopped to take a break, so I asked her if she was a student, a teacher or if she was trying her hand at self-education. "All three," she replied.

We talked for awhile, and it turned out that she was a Ph.D. and an associate professor of Health Education at a major State University. She also eagerly pointed out to me that she taught meditation and was studying for her class.

I told her that I also meditated each day on the Word of God, and we had a warm and interesting discussion about different approaches to meditation. I would like to say I changed her mind about Zen-I did not- but I did give her something to think about in her quest for peace, comfort and health.

Biblically, there is only one source of true and lasting peace, comfort and health, and that is God, the Creator of all that is. To each of us as Christians, God has granted the pleasure and the privilege of a relationship with Him. But like any relationship, we must work at maintaining and developing it.

Bible meditation is one of the best (and most enjoyable) ways of maintaining and developing our relationship with God. As we center in on His Word, He speaks to us through it; He points out to us things that are not right in our lives; He reveals spiritual truths to us; He gives us direction and guidance; and He affirms us as His children. Not only this, but as we store His Word in our hearts, He releases His power into our lives. Our lives are never the same, they are touched by the Creator of the universe.

My prayer is that you have become convinced of the benefits that a regular time of Bible meditation can bring to your life, and that you make it your daily habit. If you are not so convinced, read the book through again, study what the Scriptures have to say on the topic, talk to people who meditate daily on God's Word until you are convinced that it is what you should be doing.

And if you are convinced that you should be meditating regularly on the Word of God, then take the principles laid out in this book and adapt them to your personality and circumstances. Own them, make them your own and you can enjoy a rich, full and rewarding relationship with God.

God, help us to believe in the power of your Word. Help us to stop everyday and get quiet before your Word. Help us to be listeners—to listen to you speak to us by your mighty voice. Help us to meditate on your Word and apply it to our lives. Amen.

How to Meditate

Step 1: Choose a quiet place and interruption-free time in which to meditate.

Step 2: Pray and ask God to show you which passage of Scripture He wants you to begin meditating on.

Step 3: Think through the selected passage again and again—prayerfully.

Step 4: Apply the Word.

Step 5: Relax and enjoy the Lord.

How to Meditate

**Step 1: Choose a quiet place
and interruption-free
time in which to meditate.**

**Step 2: Pray and ask God to
show you which passage of
Scripture he wants you to begin
meditating on.**

**Step 3: Think through the selected
passage again and again—
prayerfully.**

Step 4: Apply the Word.

**Step 5: Relax and enjoy the
Lord.**

Appendices

Appendices

The thrust of this book has been Bible meditation. Since we emphasized taking only small parts of Scripture for 15-20 minutes a day of relaxed reflection, balance requires broad reading of Scripture as well. We include three appendices to help you in your personal Bible Study and further study of Bible meditation.

The first appendix is a general guide to help you in Bible reading. I emphasize four basic points in the first appendix; persistence, oral reading, review and obedience.

The second appendix is taken from my book with Rob Penner, *Grace Simply Grace*. This second appendix is a guide for people who wish to spend 30 minutes a day in Bible Study.

The third appendix is a reading list for readers who are interested in further study about meditation. I have divided this list up into Christian books dealing with meditation and medical books discussing meditation.

Appendix 1

Bible Reading

Why read the Bible? God desires His people to learn and obey His Word. For instance, "Seek and read from the Book of the Lord...."[1] The writer of the Proverbs instructs, "My son, do not forget my teaching, but let your heart keep my commandments."[2] God told Joshua, "this book of the law shall not depart out of your mouth..."[3] He was to meditate on it day and night. David praised God by saying that the book of God was put into his heart so that he would not sin.[4] The three basic reasons for these commands are for God's glory, for our good and for the evangelization of the world.

Jesus rebuked the Pharisees for their lack of Scriptural knowledge, "you know neither the Scriptures nor the power of God."[5] God's power was absent from their lives and these two symptoms of spiritual dryness (a lack of Scriptural knowledge and a lack of power) usually go hand in hand. If God's power is to be upon us, then it is necessary that we also have a clear knowledge of Scripture. Two men stand out in this respect in the Bible, Ezra and Apollos. Ezra lived in the 400's B.C. He "set his heart to study the law of God and to do it."[6]   When Nehemiah rebuilt Jerusalem's wall, Ezra was the man called upon to teach the commands of God to all the people of Judah.   Ezra's faithfulness in private reading paid off in his public usefulness in the ministry.

Likewise, Apollos is a New Testament example of a man who dedicated himself to the study of God's Word. He was called "well versed in the Scriptures."[7] Paul, the apostle, states that the Lord used Apollos to "water" what he (Paul) had planted.[8]

Jesus used the Old Testament as a guideline for His life. From this testament He found His identity as the Messianic God-Man. In dealing with Satan, Jesus took the Old Testament and did battle with the enemy. Obviously, early in His life He became thoroughly acquainted with God's oracles. As a young lad, He confounded many of the teachers of the law.

There are four essentials to successful Bible reading: (1) persistence, (2) oral reading, (3) systematic review and (4) obedience to the Word.

Persistence

History gives us several good examples of persistence.

Thomas Edison, known for his famous inventions, was strangely pleased over a failure in developing the electric light. After his 10,000th failure he exclaimed to a stunned onlooker, "Well, good, that is 10,000 ways that I know will not work."[9]

Michaelangelo asked a veteran sculptor what was the required talent to be great at his art.

"Talent is cheap; dedication is expensive; it will cost you your life,"[10] replied the old man.

Ben Franklin accomplished much through sheer persistence. Professor Robert Dick Wilson mastered 47 languages by being willing to do just a little at a time, but studying persistently.[11] The way to greatness in becoming a song writer, said a music master, was to be willing to "put the seat of your pants to the seat of your chair and keep it there until you are through."[12] Derek Prince stated that George Mueller of Bristol read the Bible through 100 times in his life by daily devotional reading. Mueller was also a devoted daily Bible meditator. Taking these examples from the men mentioned above, we can apply two principles to the reading of God's Word.

First, Bible reading does not have to be a lot at a time but simply some each day. The important thing is to read persistently and make some progress every day (even if it is only a paragraph or a half chapter)-but try not to miss a day.[13]

Second, make sure that the time of reading is a time of diligent application to the Word. Dr. Robert Dick Wilson would not allow himself to turn a page in his language grammar books until he had mastered the preceding page. Shouldn't we be equally diligent in our study of the Bible?

In ten years, lawyer Gene Neill read through the Bible more than 70 times by persistent reading of a specific number of chapters morning and night for that ten years.

Oral Reading

A second suggestion for effective Bible reading is to read it out loud. Although much is said today about speed reading, hardly anything is ever mentioned about the value of reading aloud. St. Augustine was shocked to see that Ambrosius read silently. Birger Gerhardsson wrote, "A famous case is provided by Augustine's undistinguished astonishment over the fact that Ambrosius read silently, and his attempt to explain the phenomenon."[14] This was true in the time of the New Testament as well.[15] The Ethiopian eunuch read the prophecy of Isaiah aloud when Philip the evangelist overtook him and taught him about the Messiah.[16] God told the children of Israel that His Word was to ever be on their lips. "You shall talk of them when you sit in your house, when you walk by the way, and when you lie down and when you rise."[17]

In the rabbinic tradition of ancient Israel, the rabbis were specialists in training people to remember. They forced, cajoled and coerced their students to learn material orally. They never considered the material which they had presented to their students learned until it could be quoted verbatim. "The pupil is thus duty bound to maintain his teacher's exact words."[18] The Psalms state that the responsible father was to recite the acts of God in the hearing of his son.[19]

People have asked me how I learn the location of Scripture verses. Generally, I tell them to read the Bible out loud.

Educational psychologists tell us that vocalized reading material is retained at a capacity of 200-300% greater than material read silently.

Simply applied, read the Bible out loud. Adding the first two suggestions together (persistence, oral reading) we should read the Bible aloud, every day.[20]

Review

I consider review so important that during the year I taught the Bible in a Christian High School, I made my classes review during the whole last six week period. This review produced particular and intense trial for many students. However, much lasting fruit was born at this time as well. I remembered virtually nothing from any of my high school classes and I wanted to make sure that my students did not duplicate my experience.

At the end of each day, it is wise to make a quick mental summary of what you read that day. Repetition is an important facet of review.

The Rabbi Hillel stated, "The man who repeats it one hundred times is not to be compared with the man who repeats it one hundred and one times."[21] "A rabbi's life is one continual repetition."[22]

Pastor John MacArthur discussed how he thoroughly learned the book of First John in *God's Will is Not Lost*. His method-once a day, every day for a month he read the book. This took him only 20 minutes per day. He learned the book.

> "Let me share how I study the Bible, and how the Bible has come alive to me. I began in 1 John. One day I sat down and read all five chapters straight through. It took me 20 minutes. Reading one book straight through was terrific. (The Bible

wasn't written as an assortment of good little individual verses. The Bible was written with flow and context.) The next day, I sat down and read 1 John straight through again. The third day, I sat down and read 1 John straight through. The fourth day, straight through again. The fifth day, I sat down and read it again. I did this for 30 days. Do you know what happens at the end of 30 days? You know what is in 1 John!"[23]

G. Campbell Morgan taught the Scriptures during the great revival period at the turn of the century, around 1900. He worked with such greats as Dwight Moody, Charles Spurgeon and Andrew Murray. Morgan would read a Bible book 50 times out loud before attempting to teach it.[24]

Review and repetition are indispensable facets of reading the Scriptures. This, coupled with the two previous points of persistence and oral reading, brings us to the place where we are now daily reading a portion of the Bible out loud and reviewing that portion we read on the same day. (This oral review can be done in a one sentence overview at bed time.) These three facets lead us on to our last point, which is that he who reads the Scriptures must obey them.

Obedience to the Word

"But be doers of the Word and not hearers only, deceiving yourselves."[25] King David prayed for understanding of the Scriptures.[26] Understanding precedes obedience. Jesus condemned the Pharisees for being those "who would preach but not practice"[27] the Word of God. God wants us to obey Him with understanding.

The people of Judah disobeyed Ezekiel's preaching. God said that Ezekiel was like an entertainer who "sang songs to them" and "played a musical instrument for them."[28] They did not obey him although they were entertained. For them it was sin.[29] King Zedekiah disobeyed God and it cost him greatly. He was deposed from his throne because of disobedience.[30] Abraham obeyed the Lord and the ultimate statement over Abraham's life was that "The Lord had blessed him in all things."[31] While the rest of the world suffered a flood, obedient Noah floated.

Simply put, when God speaks to you out of the Bible, obey Him.

Successful Bible Study

1. Persistence
2. Read Aloud
3. Review
4. Obey

Notes to Appendix 1

1. Isaiah 34:1
2. Proverbs 3:1
3. Joshua 1:8
4. Psalms 119:11
5. Mark 12:24
6. Ezra 7:10
7. Acts 18:24
8. 1 Corinthians 3:6
9. Jill Hardin, "Graduation Address" 1977, Tyler Street Christian Academy, Dallas, Texas.
10. *Agony and the Ecstasy*, Irving Stone,©1961, p.96. Doubleday and Company Inc. New York, New York.
11. Robert Dick Wilson was professor of Old Testament Language and Literature at Princeton Theological Seminary early in this century. Prof. E. J. Young at Westminster Theological Seminary could read 26 languages.
12. Professor James Hiles, Gordon-Conwell Theological Seminary, given at an advisee meeting in September, 1974.
13. *How to Do What you Want to Do:The Art of Self-Discipline*, ©1976.
14. *Memory and Manuscript*, Birger Gerhardsson ©1961, 1964, p. 163n.
15.Revelation 1:3
16. Acts 8:30
17. Deuteronomy 6:7
18. *Memory and Manuscript*, p.133.
19. Psalms 78:5-7.
20. *Your Memory: How It Works and How to Improve It*, Kenneth L. Higbee,©1977, p.155. Prentice- Hall Inc., Englewood Cliffs, New Jersey.
21. Birger Gerhardsson, Ibid, p. 134.
22. Ibid, p. 163n.
23. *God's Will Is Not Lost*, John MacArthur Jr. ©1973, p. 16. Victor Books, Wheaton, Illinois.

24. *G. Campbell Morgan, The Man and His Ministry*, John Harries, © 1930, p. 199. Public Domain, Fleming Revell Publishers.
25. James 1:22
26. Psalms 119:34
27. Matthew 23:3
28. Ezekiel 33:30-33.
29. James 4:17
30. Jeremiah 34.
31. Genesis 24:1

Appendix 2
30 Minutes of Bible Study Each Day

Decide on a book of the Bible that you want to study for one month. Before you begin, purchase a folder to store all your insights from your study, and write down all that you know about the book that you plan to study.

Day 1

Read the book through in one sitting, rapidly, aloud.

Day 2

Read the book through again, and write down the *big idea* of the book.

Day 3

Read the book through again, looking for repeated words or phrases. Write down these words or phrases, then ask why the author uses them. Record your work.

Day 4

Ask *who*. Write down all the people mentioned. Which ones are the main characters? Who are these people? Why are they important? Are they mentioned anywhere else in the Bible? Check your concordance. What have you learned about these people? Summarize your thoughts.

Day 5

Ask *where*. List the geographical locations. Which ones are important in understanding this book? Find these locations on a map. If they are cities, pick one or two and read about them in a Bible dictionary. If they are countries, choose one or two and read about them in a Bible dictionary. Think about how this information helps you understand the book. Write down your ideas.

Day 6

Ask *when*. Look for words that indicate time: *before, after, while, during, then, no longer, as long as,* etc. This should help you see the sequence of events. What happened in the past? What is taking place presently? What are future events?

Day 7

Ask *what*. What events are taking place in this book? What topics are discussed? Write down your answers.

Day 8

Observe and record contrasts. These can be broad contrasts, such as two contrasting characters, contrasting events, or contrasting themes. They can be less broad, being contrasts within a paragraph and identified by the conjunction, *but*.

Day 9

What illustrations does the author use? Are they from everyday life situations, from Scripture, from past history, or from personal experiences?

Day 10

Write down any words or terms that you don't understand. Go through the following steps to discover what words mean:

1. How is the word or phrase used in this book? Write down anything you learn from its use in each passage. Consider the context of the passage. What is this passage talking about? How does the main idea of this passage help you understand the word or phrase? Consider this for

every passage where the word is used in the book you are studying.

2. How does the author use the same word or phrase in other books? Use a concordance to help you find this information.

3. Look the word up in a concordance, and check the original Greek or Hebrew. (The introduction to the concordance will tell you how to do such exercises.)

4. If you have a word-study book, look the word up in that book.

5. Look up the passage in a commentary, and see if anything is mentioned about the word or phrase.

6. Ask someone else for their insights.

7. Look up the word in your native-language dictionary.

8. Read the passage in another translation.

9. Formulate your definition of the word or phrase, then insert it into the passage to see if it makes sense. Do you now understand the passage?

Day 11

Do the same as Day 10. Finish the work for Day 10, or find the meaning for another word or term.

Day 12

If the book is 6 chapters or less, write a brief summary of each paragraph. If the book is more than 6 chapters, then write a brief chapter summary.

Day 13

Think through each paragraph and ask this question: How does each paragraph lead into the next? Does the following paragraph continue on the same topic or does it change topics, characters, ideas, or events? How does the paragraph fit with the overall message, the big idea of the book?

Can you discover how the author has organized his material? How is the material organized: biographically, geographically, chronologically, logically, or thematically?

Does the author answer a series of questions? Does he move from a problem to the solution, from general to specifics, from theology to practical application? (If you are working with a book with more than 6 chapters, you may want to go chapter by chapter for Day 13.)

Day 14 and Day 15

Continue working through Day 13.

Day 16 and Day 17

Consider historical background. How did the original audience receive and understand this book?

1. If the book is a letter to a church, answer the following questions:

a. When was the church founded? Can you find any information in the book of Acts? Consult a Bible dictionary.

b. Who founded the church? What kind of reception did these original evangelists receive?

c. Read through the letter and discover the church's strengths and weaknesses.

d. Imagine what it would be like to be a member of this church.

e. What is the prevailing religion in the area? What religious beliefs did these Christians have prior to their conversion?

f. Are there any customs or cultural insights that would

be helpful to know? Do some reading in outside sources.

2. If the book is an historical narrative:

a. What was happening in Israel's (or the early church's) history before and after this book?

b. What was happening in the surrounding cultures?

c. How does this book fit into the overall history of God's people?

3. If the book is one of the Prophets:

a. When did this prophet minister?

b. What was going on in Israel's history at that time?

c. Who received the prophecy?

Day 18

Ask the literary question: What type of literature is being used in the whole book, or the passage under consideration?

The first distinction is to determine whether the passage is prose or poetry. Poetry uses figures of speech and is not to be interpreted literally. Learn to recognize the following types of literature. Read about them in a Bible dictionary or encyclopedia. Understand their specific characteristics so you interpret correctly.

1. Epistles: the New Testament letter form; composed of various parts

2. Gospels

3. Parables

4. Oracles: found in the Prophets

5. Didactic literature: having the purpose of teaching

6. Apocalyptic literature. Examples: Revelation, parts of Isaiah, Ezekiel, Daniel, and Zechariah.

7. Historical narrative: literature which traces the history of Israel or the Church

8. Wisdom literature: found in Proverbs and Ecclesiastes. It is also very important for you to read up on Hebrew poetry so you can understand the Psalms and the Prophets.

Day 19

Meditate on either the whole book or a certain passage. Just spend today thinking about the book. Write down your insights.

Day 20

Finish anything you haven't completed, or decide for yourself what study you want to do today.

Day 21

Observe progression. Does the author move to a climax of ideas, emotion, or story line? Does he move from specific to general? From a question to the answer? From a statement to an illustration? From teaching to application? Observe and record your insights and then ask: Why?

Day 22

Wrestle with a difficult passage. Read through the passage several times. Meditate on the passage. Bombard the passage with why questions. Answer the why questions that you asked. Consider the context and main ideas of the surrounding paragraphs. How does this difficult passage fit into the overall message of the book? Write down your conclusions and ask yourself if this is a reasonable interpretation. Does it go against any major truth or teaching of the Bible? Ask someone else their opinion of this passage.

Day 23

Discover the author's main concern.

What does he want the readers to know and understand? What are the readers' main concerns? Have they asked certain questions that the author is answering? Write down what you discover.

Day 24

Read the whole book through again in one sitting. Think once again about the overall message of the book.

Day 25

Bombard the text with why questions. Write out your questions, then try to answer them. Is the answer found somewhere in the book? Just sit back and think for a while; sometimes the answer just involves allowing yourself time to think. Be sure to write down your answers; don't consider them unimportant. Share your ideas with someone else.

Day 26

Same as Day 25

Day 27

Summarize the basic truths of the book. Ask yourself how these truths apply to your life in the twentieth century. Does the book: Teach me something I don't know? Bring correction? Bring encouragement? Help me understand more about God or mankind?

Day 28

In light of these truths (what you wrote for day 27), ask, "What changes need to take place in my life? Am I to change what I believe? Am I to change in my relationships with others? Am I to change in my relationship with God?" Try and personalize the book into your life. Write down your answers.

Day 29

What truths or applications could you make from this book if you were teaching it? Write them out.

Day 30

Pray through the application process. Write out your prayer as a permanent record of your application.

Review what you wrote about the book before you began your study, and be encouraged with your progress. Store all your questions and answers in a file. Now ... decide what book you will study next.

Appendix 3

Suggested Reading List

Christian Books Pertaining to Meditation:
1. *Alone with God*, Campbell McAlpine.
2. *Meditating on the Word*, Dietrich Bonhoeffer.
3. *Adrenalin and Stress*, Archibald Hart.
4. *Eternity in Their Hearts*, Don Richardson.
5. *Voices from the Edge of Eternity*, Don Myers.
6. *The Confessions*, St. Augustine of Hippo.
6. *The Pursuit of God*, A.W. Tozer.
8. *How to Be Filled with the Holy Spirit*, A.W. Tozer.
9. *Waiting on God*, Andrew Murray.
10. *A Few Things I Learned Since I knew it All*, Jerry Cook.

Medical Books Discussing Meditation:
1. *The Relaxation Response*, Herbert Benson M.D.
2. *Beyond the Relaxation Response,* Herbert Benson M.D.
3. *Stress, Diet and Your Heart*, Dean Ornish M.D.
4. *Head First*, Norm Cousins.
5. *Mind as Healer, Mind as Slayer*, Kenneth Pelletier M.D.
6. *Minding the Body, Mending the Mind*, Joan Borysenko M.D.
7. *The Stress of Life*, Hans Selye M.D.
8. *Meditating for Success*, Paul Meier M.D.